D0207798

NEW RULERS
in the ghetto

RECENT TITLES IN CONTRIBUTIONS IN AFRO-AMERICAN AND AFRICAN STUDIES
Series Adviser: *HOLLIS R. LYNCH*

NEW RULERS
in the ghetto

THE COMMUNITY DEVELOPMENT CORPORATION AND URBAN POVERTY

HARRY EDWARD BERNDT

CONTRIBUTIONS IN AFRO-AMERICAN
AND AFRICAN STUDIES, NUMBER 28

GREENWOOD PRESS
WESTPORT, CONNECTICUT
LONDON, ENGLAND

Library of Congress Cataloging in Publication Data

Berndt, Harry Edward.
New rulers in the ghetto.

(Contributions in Afro-American and African studies ; no. 28)
Bibliography: p.
Includes index.
1. Community development corporations—United States. 2. Community development—United States. I. Title. II. Series.
HC110.P63B44 1977   352   76-47888
ISBN 0-8371-9399-0

Library of Congress Catalog Card Number: 76-47888
ISBN 0-8371-9399-0

First published in 1977

Greenwood Press, Inc.
51 Riverside Avenue, Westport, Connecticut 06880

Printed in the United States of America

TO

NANCY PFEIL BERNDT,
my wife and friend of twenty-five years;
and to
LESLIE,
ROBIN,
ERIC,
and
COLIN,
our children

TABLES

ACKNOWLEDGMENTS

A number of friends provided encouragement and criticism while I worked on this manuscript. John Ainley, John Alt, Roberta Arnold, Melvin Oliver, and Dr. Dennis Brun read and criticized the early drafts of the beginning chapters. Nesby Moore, Jr., of Union Sarah Economic Development Corporation (USEDC) gave permission to use corporate data and records, without which this work would not have been possible. I am also grateful to Horace Browder, the former director of Administration for USEDC, who verified matters of finance and corporate history, and to Bennie Crawford, my secretary, who cheerfully assisted in preparing the early drafts. Also, thanks are due Professor George Rawick for his encouragement and assistance in preparing the final drafts.

To Professor Richard Ratcliff of Washington University of St. Louis I extend special thanks for his constant criticism and many suggestions. Dr. Ratcliff read the manuscript in its entirety a number of times and offered both editorial and substantive suggestions. He was a good friend throughout and, although very busy with other work, always took time to be helpful.

All errors, of course, are mine.

St. Louis, Missouri
May 12, 1976

part 1
THE COMMUNITY ECONOMIC DEVELOPMENT CORPORATION

INTRODUCTION

This work focuses on community development and its effectiveness as one officially defined response to poverty in urban areas of the United States.

First produced in 1967, the community development corporation (CDC) is the vehicle for community development under current federal antipoverty programs. By definition and stated intent, the CDC is a community-controlled corporation established to improve the quality of life for the poor—in specifically defined geographic areas—by creating the means to provide jobs and income for the community. The CDC makes use of a variety of strategies, including the acquisition of existing businesses, the development of new businesses, investment in the physical assets of the community, assistance through loans and technical service to community entrepreneurs, and participation with private sector interests in joint ventures. Its avowed objective "is to break the cycle of poverty in low-income communities by arresting tendencies toward dependency, chronic unemployment, and community deterioration".[1]

There are rural as well as urban CDCs; the rural ones are significantly different from the urban, particularly in the meaning of community. This work deals only with the urban CDCs that have been created and funded by the Office of Economic Opportunity (OEO)—now called the Community Services Administration—through legislation calling for a Special Impact Program (SIP).[2]

The legislation, passed in 1964 that created SIP provides for a cooperative effort among the community, the federal government, and the private business sector. The CDCs' primary base is designed to be in a poor community that contributes the human and physical resources as well as the overall direction to the program. The federal government's role is to grant major funding and technical assistance, along with preferential consideration on contracts. Finally, the private sector is supposed to participate through membership on the CDCs' boards of directors, provision of technical assistance, partnership in joint ventures, grants and loans, and creation of sheltered markets for CDC ventures.

While the concept of the CDC is often viewed as an innovation of the 1960s, it is an outgrowth of ideas that have shaped "poverty programs" at least since the early nineteenth century. Robert Owen's villages of cooperation were forerunners of today's CDCs, both in philosophy and expected outcome. Owen suggested that the poor be placed in specially designated areas, be given an initial capital grant from taxes, and be expected to make their own way through self-discipline and hard work. This proposal was consistent with ideas of the time that poverty was a serious social problem that could be solved by programs of aid to the poor. These programs were designed not to distribute the wealth, but rather to help the poor help themselves. Hence, the poor would be taught the skills necessary to make them useful citizens and to enable them to fully participate in and enjoy the benefits of capitalist society. The underlying theory was that poverty existed because of the poor's limited opportunities as well as their own faults and failures, and not because of any defects in the economic and social system.

Self-help has always been a major factor in poverty programs. Advocates of self-help explicitly deny or ignore an opposing view that, in order to eliminate poverty, the system needs to be restructured. They see no need for structural change because, they believe, the poor are poor through their own fault. The self-help concept is solidly grounded in the work ethic which states that to work is a virtue and not to work is a crime. In a sense, then, self-help has always been a form of work enforcement, whether sponsored by the state through the workhouse or by a charitable group through its workshop or farm. The Salvation Army, for example, was active in nineteenth-century London providing food and shelter, in return for which the poor worked in the Army's factories, workshops, and laundries. During the great depression, the unemployed in Chickasha, Oklahoma, were permitted to scrape food left on restaurant plates on the condition that they chop wood donated by farmers.[3] Thus, the general thesis of self-help has been that the poor need assistance in gaining the capabilities to "make it" in the existing system. If they remain poor, they simply do not have the personal qualities to be other than destitute.

From the beginning, the pattern of poverty and the solutions offered for it in the United States resembled those in England and Europe. In the first place, the settlers brought with them many of the institutions and attitudes of the countries they had left. The European idea that the majority of people were poor through their own fault was reinforced by the "super individualism" of the frontiersman, hunter, and mariner.

The ideas of self-help and the work ethic were widely disseminated even among the several million blacks in America who had suffered the burdens of slavery for centuries. These ideas were encouraged by the experiences of the few blacks who were able to achieve some measure of independence and social status. Prior to the Civil War, the free black had a near monopoly on menial and semiskilled occupations such as barber, chef, house servant, and brick maker. He was convinced that only hard work and thrift could give him moderate safety in the hostile society in which he lived.

The slave had little to say about his work or his future, but white abolitionists and others were interested in both—work from a concern over what the slave would do when free and the future as it related to freedom. This concern manifested itself in programs for the improvement of blacks, fashioned after white ideas of culture and work. They generally taught self-help and centered on the practical matters of everyday living. One of the most important program models called for the establishment of all-black communities, in which blacks would have control over community resources and gain practical experience in managing their own affairs.

Following emancipation and the Civil War, blacks were urged by their leaders to work hard, save their money, and enter business. The capitalistic system and free enterprise were extolled as the mainsprings of freedom, without which all but a few would be forced back into slavery. Booker T. Washington, the first important postslavery leader and a proponent of capitalism, encouraged blacks to learn a trade or save for a farm. He believed that the seminal stage for financial success was to be found in either the trades or agriculture. He also encouraged the development of all-black towns, which he believed would provide the basis for equality with whites. (As a modern parallel to Washington's position, one of the arguments supporting the CDC concept is that integration can be forwarded by placing blacks in management positions in the CDC, negotiating on equal terms with whites from established corporations.)

Following Washington, W. E. B. DuBois and Marcus Garvey emphasized self-help through education and business development. DuBois's "talented tenth" thesis espoused concentrating on the elite of black youth, whom he envisioned as able to move into responsible government and business positions. They would be the vanguard for the uplift of the race. Garvey's Universal Negro Improvement Association (UNIA) was oriented toward business and was based on the belief that blacks could achieve parity with whites only through capitalism. Garvey believed that anyone who opposed capitalism also opposed human advancement. The UNIA approach to establishing all-black businesses is part of the tradition from which the CDC evolved. Washington, DuBois, and Garvey were important early influences on today's black acceptance of the CDC philosophy.

With the advent of the depression, the Hoover administration continued to emphasize the virtues of self-help, equality of opportunity, and sturdy individualism. Hoover refused to bring the weight of federal support to the relief of the poor. He encouraged voluntary cooperative activity by big business, trade associations, local communities, and charitable groups. Not until Franklin Roosevelt was elected president did the federal government become involved with the problems of the poor and unemployed, and his program also followed the tradition of self-help. The Civilian Conservation Corporation, the Agriculture Adjustment Act, the Home Owners Loan Act, and the Works Project Administration were all designed to help those who would help themselves. They reflected the philosophy of American capitalism, individualism, and the work ethic. The premise behind the New Deal legislation was not that there was anything wrong with the system, but rather that more people needed to become involved in it.

The next aggressive effort by the federal government specifically designed to assist the poor did not occur until the 1960s. The seminal programs started under the Kennedy administration's New Frontier and the Johnson administration's Great Society and its associated War on Poverty. The programs created during this period involved programs for employment, education, health service, and legal aid among others. The program from which the CDCs evolved was the Community Action Program (CAP).[4] The purpose of the CAP was to organize the poor to work on their own behalf. Self-help would help diminish the feelings of powerlessness thought to pervade the poor communities. The poor were supposed to know best what their problems were and with adequate federal help would find ways to solve them.

The major emphasis of CAP was on community control. It was this factor more than any other that carried over into the CDCs. The theoretical base for CDC was a twofold one: community control and the community, rather than the individual, as the recipient of benefits. According to the theory, the individual would benefit from the development of the community. Through the development of community institutions, the ownership and renovation of community physical assets, and the acquisition and development of community business, the quality of life and life chances of the individual would improve, and better housing and employment would be made available. Therefore, the focus of CDC was on the community as client.

If the community (i.e., the poor community which is assumed to be the best judge of needs) is the client, it follows that the community should control the program. Otherwise, someone other than the client would determine the community's needs. Advocates of the CDC concept are in agreement on this point, and arguments favoring community control are dominant in CDC literature. Community control is seen to be necessary for the proper functioning of the CDC and to be the major factor responsible for deriving ancillary benefits. For example, Stewart Perry believes that the cause of integration will advance as a result of the black community's opportunity to interact with outside groups while representing community interests. This integration is possible only when the community controls its own institutions.[5] Geoffrey Faux makes the same observation: "The establishment of black business increases the amount of real integration in the nation by creating situations in which both parties bargain as equals."[6] Faux also argues that with community control programs are more flexible and responsive to local needs than when they are designed in Washington.[7] Finally, Alan Altshuler states that community control is probably the most feasible major demand that blacks are making, and that community control might enhance the legitimacy of the system in their eyes.[8] Community control, then, is meant to provide the core of community self-help and to insure that the poor define community problems and their solutions. It is to be a vehicle through which the poor can gain experience in positions of control and responsibility as members of boards of directors, as managers, and as problem-solvers.

A recent book by Charles Hampden-Turner, *From Poverty to Dignity,* is even more effusive in describing the benefits of community control and of other aspects of the CDC.[9] Since this work is one of the more important positive ones on the CDC, it is worth critical attention here.

In Hampden-Turner's earlier book, *Radical Man,* he establishes ten principles of development for the self-actualized or radical person. He defines the radical person as one who defies authority, or would defy authority, in response to a belief in a higher morality. In *From Poverty to Dignity,* Hampden-Turner applies his psychological paradigm of the radical person to blacks and the poor, and finally it becomes a model for the CDC.

Although Hampden-Turner is concerned with all the poor in the United States, he applies his principles of development to blacks first and his analysis begins with the conflict between the races. While he later includes all poor in his analysis, he uses the terms *poor* and *black* almost interchangeably. We will follow his lead, as most of the urban CDCs involve black poor people, and this work concerns only the urban CDCs.

Basic to Hampden-Turner's argument is his concept of the radical poor. He argues that for the poor to gain relative equality with the white middle class, they must as a group become the radical person. They must reorganize their existence to permit them to live for themselves: "Such radicalism requires neither violence nor the taking of every proposition to some ultimate extreme. It requires that the poor, and especially poor minorities, have the right to reorganize their existence from the roots up, and that the dominant white society respond to such new conceptions."[10] This concept of the radical poor is unique in its strong inference that "radical" depends on permission from the dominant class, that is, that the poor have "the right" as understood by established society. Hampden-Turner believes that the poor will become radical as a result of the synergistic action of social opposites in a dialectic relationship. He defines synergy as "the fusion between different human aims and resources to create more between the interacting parties than they had prior to the interaction."[11] His concept of the radical poor, it would seem, differs from his concept of radical man in that, rather than defy authority (as the radical man would), they should seek a resynthesis, a compromise that will be beneficial to both parties to the dialectic.

After applying his ten principles of development to the poor, Hampden-Turner attempts an application to the community development corporation. If the application for an individual represents interpersonal dynamics, then that for a group might best be described as organizational dynamics or organizational interaction.

With regard to community control, Hampden-Turner states that the institution and its structure are created from the experience of the creating group, and that this experience provides a bridge between the group and the institution. His analysis suggests that the CDC, through its policy and structure, reflects what can be identified as a uniquely community-oriented organization. The CDC differs from other organizations—for example, other manufacturers or profit-making organizations—in its goal of creating the greatest possible benefits for the community, and not simply of maximizing profits.

The question must be asked whether Hampden-Turner's analysis is based on the ideology of the CDC movement or the reality of the CDC in practice. Hampden-Turner argues that the CDC, because of community commitment and community control, will provide more meaningful employment for the poor than the normal corporate employer will, and that it will reinvest the organization's profits into socially beneficial projects. He suggests that the poor, in their efforts to improve themselves and their community, have a different value system, a higher morality, than that of the majority population. There is a strong inference in his work that hierarchical relationships will somehow be softened if community people assume supervisory positions, and that the negative aspects of the ghetto, such as higher insurance rates, high crime rates, inadequate transportation, and depleted market conditions, will not prove fatal to community-controlled business.

Hampden-Turner defines the concept of free existence to mean freedom from economic domination by those outside the community. Free existence would result from the surplus value created by the neighborhood organization and its members for the benefit of the community. Only through using their own resources is this freedom possible. He believes that the community understands the truth of this concept. The community would remain free of outside money and techniques because "it is absurd to think that any poor community, surrounded by affluence, can be developed through the desire of its members for outside money and techniques."[12] Since CDCs are funded organizations, and they seek money from whatever source available, i.e., from government, private foundations, corporations, and individuals, and a major CDC policy is to seek technical assistance from private corporations, Hampden-Turner's position is clearly contrary to reality.

One of Hampden-Turner's principles of development, identity, requires that the organization provide high-quality role structures, a sense of rootedness, and mobility. Hampden-Turner believes that the CDC greatly expands occupational role opportunities for community residents. In comparing the CDCs with the Community Action Programs (CAPs), he concludes that where the CAPs failed to create new roles for the poor the CDCs have succeeded. He attributes this difference to the CAPs' dependency on federal funding. Hampden-Turner makes the following observation on the CDCs' success in attaining identity:

> The industrial model combined with an organized cultural and political base provides roles for president, directors, board members, staff helpers, brothers, organizers, block leaders, workers and a host of social functions. All such roles could be attained by poor persons in a relatively short time, and there is considerable lateral and upward mobility within and between CDCs and their coordinating center, the National Congress for Community Economic Development in Washington.[13]

Whether the CDCs have created employment opportunities for community residents at the level indicated by Hampden-Turner is questionable. This question will be taken up later in this book.

Together with Stewart Perry and Geoffrey Faux, Hampden-Turner sees the CDC as a means by which blacks can integrate with whites through business interaction. All three writers posit that in business transactions people bargain as equals. Because blacks would represent an equal level of management in a business environment, both a model for increasing integration and an example of black competence would be provided. Whether or not the level of participation can be expected to halt the rapid resegregation occurring in the United States is not discussed. The Kerner Report of 1968 predicted that the black population of the central cities would reach 20.3 million people by 1983, an increase of 68 percent from the 1968 figure.[14]

For Hampden-Turner, the concept of social marketing is the culminating agent for the CDC's social impact. Through social marketing and the CDC, he believes that the poor will be able to harness the energy of their greatest allies—the middle-class whites who have expressed a commitment to social justice and need only a means to express their commitment. Social marketing will offer these people the opportunity to purchase products not only for utility but also to benefit the poor directly:

> The CDCs can present themselves as a source of new life styles, as pioneers in a new conception of fighting poverty, as redefiners of the very terms wealth, excellence, social responsibility, justice, etc. When they meet and negotiate with others, they will have defined the subject matter, shaped the agenda, and listed the priorities. There are infinite degrees of freedom and choice for a poor community. They can choose to employ welfare recipients, rehabilitated convicts, help mental patients, extol Black Power, rebuild the ghetto, fight racial injustice, build free schools, create safe streets— the list is limited only by the limits of imagination within the CDC and among responding customers, and by the amount of activity that can be subsumed beneath the supply of each increment of a product or service.[15]

Hampden-Turner believes that by tying products to causes such as these CDCs can gain the adherents of the causes as customers, thus increasing profits. Further, the CDCs can advance their own best interests by gaining support for those causes most beneficial to their communities. Furthermore, the competition will find it very difficult to cope with such programs since their products will offer only utility. "What can a corporate chairman with three houses and two swimming pools do about a CDC which says it needs the money more than he does?"[16]

In addition to attracting consumers to purchase the products the CDC produces and sells, Hampden-Turner suggests the possibility of encouraging other producers and sellers to forego profits for the cause of social justice. "A CDC could run a Social Justice Book Club, pressing those authors who hawk their social conscience to waive royalties on books sold to the club, and encouraging their publishers to be similarly generous."[17]

Finally, Hampden-Turner believes that, with the assistance of its consumer allies, the CDC movement could effectively change the course of national policy.

> Had there been a CDC source of supply when half a million marched in Washington, had the marchers broken up into buying demonstrations, switching their patronage away from those who opportunistically fueled the war machine, the war would have been over in months. CDCs would today be recognized "peace organizations," teaching the arts of conflict resolution at the community level, and exemplifying the advantage of having a corporation whose owners are visible and responsive to social demands.[18]

With its advantages both in forwarding causes and selling products, social marketing has become a strategic tool for the CDCs. Whether it could ever be as effective as Hampden-Turner envisions is debatable, however. A more important question is whether the CDC concept, or any concept, can be presented in a manner so far removed from the reality of the present. It seems that such a presentation can only damage the credibility of the advocate position.

The following chapters will describe the CDCs as they are and will raise questions about the validity of community control, the effectiveness of CDCs as creators of profit, and their impact on community employment. CDC's future potential will be presented from the perspective of present reality. Private sector and government participation, resident employment, and developing businesses for and by the poor are discussed based on the history of the CDC experience.

The material that follows grew out of my experience as director of Venture Formation and Management with a CDC during 1971-1976. In this position, I examined at first hand the validity of the CDC concept. In the day-by-day operation I observed the degree of community control in at least one major urban CDC and tested the extent of private sector participation. I was able to examine in-depth one attempt to implement the idea that the quality of life for poor people can be significantly improved by the application of economic development techniques within an urban community. In addition, my work allowed me the opportunity to observe the larger CDC picture, as it brought me into continuous contact through site visits, meetings, and literature with most of the other major CDCs. Indeed, it soon became obvious that the problems of one CDC were the same that were besetting all other CDCs.

NOTES

1. National Advisory Council on Economic Development, *Sixth Annual Report* (June 1973), p. 10.

2. Special Impact Program was the name given to the economic development efforts of OEO. Specific geographic areas were defined to establish CDCs for the purpose of making a special economic impact on those areas.

Although OEO is now known as the Community Services Administration, we will retain the use of OEO throughout, unless specifically noted, in order to lessen the likelihood of confusion.

3. Frances Fox Piven and Richard A. Cloward, *Regulating the Poor: The Functions of Public Welfare* (New York: Random House, 1971), p. 49.

4. The OEO designated areas for Community Action Agencies (CAA) for the establishment of community corporations to administer the categorical grant programs established by Congress. These programs became known under the general umbrella of the Community Action Program (CAP).

5. Stewart E. Perry, "Black Institutions, Black Separatism, and Ghetto Economic Development," *Human Organizations* 31, No. 3 (Fall 1972): 271-279.

6. Gerson Green and Geoffrey Faux, "The Social Utility of Black Enterprise," *Black Economic Development,* eds. William Haddad and Doublas Pugh (Englewood Cliffs, N.J.: Prentice Hall, 1969), p. 26.

7. Geoffrey Faux, *CDCs: New Hope for the Inner City* (New York: The Twentieth Century Fund, 1971), p. 4.

8. Alan A. Altshuler, *Community Control: The Black Demand for Participation in Large American Cities* (New York: Pegasus, 1970), p. 197.

9. Charles Hampden-Turner, *From Poverty to Dignity* (Garden City, N.Y.: Anchor Books, 1975).

10. Ibid., p. 6.

11. Ibid., p. 32.

1
FREE ENTERPRISE AND THE POOR: AN HISTORICAL PERSPECTIVE

The English settlers in North America brought with them English common law, customs, and attitudes toward work and the poor. In addition, during the colonial period a special emphasis on the individual evolved. This individualism was reinforced by popular concepts of the frontiersman, hunter, and mariner, and it "demanded that the independence and separateness of the individual be obtained at all costs."[1] In the United States, the dominant political-economic concept is still equality of opportunity, which emphasizes the importance of the individual.

It is not surprising, then, that the colonies, and later the states in America, enacted poor laws modeled on those in England.[2] The charitable organizations, mostly churches, that were called upon "in seasons of distress" by the overseers of the poor[3] also closely resembled those in England. However, in America a dimension not present in England, a dimension adding to the complexities of an already difficult problem was the existence of several million black slaves.

To understand the CDC concept, the history of the black man in America and the effect of his history on that concept must be understood. White attempts either to improve the condition of the black man or to rid the country of him, as well as thoughts on the black man as expressed by black leaders, must also be considered.

In the period before the Civil War, from the 1830s on, the white abolitionists sparked a movement to improve the condition of the free black man and to prepare for the eventual freedom of the slaves. This effort was not really a part of the abolitionist movement but developed more or less concurrent with it. While some white abolitionists were involved, colonizationists, various religionists, and antislavery groups also participated in it. Most of these groups, though opposed to slavery, wanted to rid the country of blacks. This diverse movement was concerned with making the black, free or slave, a contributing member of society, or better, a member of another society.

One concern was expressed by the black abolitionist Frederick Douglass in an editorial in the *Liberator.* The editorial, addressed to free blacks, was prompted by an increase of white immigrants who were taking jobs formerly held by blacks. For Douglass, the situation had reached a point where the actual survival of some blacks was at stake:

Learn Trades or Starve!
White men are becoming house servants, cooks and stewards on vessels—at hotels—they are becoming porters, stevedores, wood sawyers, hod carriers, brick makers, white washers, and barbers, so that blacks can scarcely find the means of subsistence—a few years ago, and a white barber would have been a curiosity—now their poles stand on every street. Now colored men, what do you mean to do, for you must do something? The American Colonization Society tells you to go to Canada. Others tell you to go to work; and to work you must go or die.[4]

Douglass' recommendation to "go to work" was not new. This answer to the black man runs throughout American history from at least the 1830s to the present day, just as it has been proposed for the poor in general in England and the United States.

Other answers were proposed. One held that the black man was indeed inferior, but that he was capable of improvement. The black could never rise to the level of the white man, but he could attain a general improvement conforming to the white man's culture.

One effort that was designed to give practical experience to blacks in managing their own affairs was the establishment of all-black communities both in the United States and elsewhere. By slavery's end, there were over 150 of these communities located in Canada, Ohio, Illinois, Indiana, and Michigan. Reformers of that period maintained that the most practical way of approaching the problem of the blacks was to provide "a positive program of training, education, and practical experience in independent, self-reliant social, economic, and political life" through the creation of these communities.[5]

These black communities were similar to European communes established during the same period in that they were highly organized internally. Also like the European communes, they provided mutual aid to members of the community and a common front to the outside world. However, whereas the European commune was in the tradition of socialism and communism, the black communities were modeled on middle-class America, particularly in their capitalistic socioeconomic philosophy. "The function of the communities, in brief, was to train the Negro for complete freedom. Time and time again the point was made that in the organized communities the Negros [*sic*] could learn to be free, learn how to earn their way in a free American society, and learn the virtues and the morals as well as the customs and mores of American society."[6] These communities were to provide the training ground needed to prepare blacks for participation in American society or in a society modeled on that in America. They were primarily designed to teach agricultural and mechanical skills in the tradition of American capitalism.

Those who supported this concept widely believed that only in a separate environment, away from the infringement of whites, could blacks really learn to cope with independence. Typical is an observation by Horace Mann:

> I have looked with great interest upon the colored settlements,
> or colonies, in Canada, in which the whites do not obtrude,
> and thrust aside the blacks, and sieze [*sic*] upon all the posts
> of honor, and all the lucrative branches of business. As mem-
> bers of such communities, the blacks will be compelled to think
> for themselves, to act independently, and to qualify themselves

and their children for the various offices and occupations which an independent community necessitates.[7]

Certainly not all efforts were meant to facilitate the absorbtion of blacks into the mainstream of society. An example was the experimental community of Nashoba, which was founded by Frances Wright. Her program called for the purchase of slaves with money raised from Southern slaveholders and for their training for freedom and colonization outside the United States. With her belief in the inherent inferiority of blacks, Wright reflected the views of the American Colonization Society. Nashoba was considered a utopian cooperative community. The care of its infirm and of its children was cooperative, and many of its activities, such as agriculture, were communitarian. It was still, however, in every sense individualistic and capitalistic. "Even as a member of a cooperative society, the Nashoba Negro was responsible for earning enough money to pay his own way at Nashoba, to purchase his own freedom and to pay the cost of his eventual colonization."[8] Nashoba eventually failed because of poor management and because it was an ill-conceived idea, i.e., colonization rather than freedom within the American society.

Other attempts at black community were Augustus Wattles' Carthagena settlement, the Refugee Home Society settlements, and the famous Port Royal experiment of the South Carolina Sea Islands. The Port Royal experiment originated during the Civil War from the Union Army's need to deal with slaves left behind on property abandoned by fleeing masters or crossing behind Union lines to escape their masters. It was the first government-sponsored settlement and one of the most complex and sophisticated of all attempts at black community.

The Port Royal experiment made it clear that the only answer to the plight of the freed slaves was federal involvement. Across the South the Union Army was attempting to deal with a daily stream of refugees who had to have shelter, clothes, medicine, and food. Some of the army commanders refused responsibility and returned the newly freed men to their masters. Others, with the help of charitable organizations in the North, attempted to cope with the large number of blacks entering their lines.

One of the first such attempts was the contraband camp created by General Benjamin Butler. These camps attempted to provide employment and social welfare for the fugitive slaves and to furnish them with clothing and tools. An army chaplain, John Eaton, was placed in charge of the administration of this program. Eaton found employment for the blacks by hiring them out to private citizens who were contracted to provide minimal maintenance for the blacks, equal to that provided by the army. Those who were not hired out to work for private citizens were put to work on confiscated plantations. The cotton was sold to the army quartermaster, and the proceeds were expended, along with charitable donations, for the benefit of the newly freed blacks.

The system of contraband camps was obviously only a stopgap measure and, in any case, could not survive the ending of the conflict. Nevertheless, many people saw the need for a continuing federal program, and in 1865 Congress passed legislation creating the Freedmen's Bureau.

The Freedmen's Bureau was one of the most successful of all government experiments in welfare and economic development. In its few years of existence, it at least temporarily protected blacks from reenslavement; it provided much needed relief to the destitute, both black and white; it enforced civil rights; and it created schools on all levels for almost every need, from elementary to university and from trade school to professional school. A paragraph from Bennett's *Before the Mayflower* provides some insight into the scope and breadth of this federal undertaking:

> This bureau, the first federal welfare agency, did the work
> of Hercules in building bridges from slavery to freedom.
> During its short life (1865-72), the Freedmen's Bureau was
> an Urban League, CIO, WPA, and Rosenwald Foundation
> all rolled into an early NAACP. It stood between the freed-
> man and the wrath of his ex-master. It gave direct medical aid
> to some one million freedmen, established hospitals, and
> distributed over twenty-one million rations, many of them to
> poverty-stricken whites. The bureau also established day schools,
> night schools and industrial schools. Practically all the Negro
> colleges (Howard, Fisk, and Moorehouse) were founded or
> received substantial financial aid from the bureau.[9]

The very success of the bureau in advocating the welfare of blacks mitigated against its survival. The bureau stimulated opposition from business and industry, racists, conservatives, and so on. It attacked the problems of poverty head on through direct relief rather than circuitously through self-help. Therefore, it was open to the traditional attacks that idleness was encouraged and that the able-bodied took advantage of aspects of the program designed for the destitute. An additional factor in its demise was that businessmen, like their English forebearers, wanted these newly released agricultural workers to be governed by the "natural law" of supply and demand. Business-minded critics stated that "the freedmen should be treated at once as any other free men. There should not be, directly or indirectly, any statutory rate of wages. There should be no interference between the hirers and the hired."[10] These opponents were soon able to cripple the program. Most of the bureau's activities ended in 1869, although its educational efforts were permitted to continue until 1872.

The Freedmen's Bureau was more directly problem-oriented than any welfare program before or since in that it defined specific problem areas and attacked them directly. The bureau's programs brought immediate aid and comfort to the poor and homeless. But in providing categorical assistance in all areas except in education, the protective nature of that assistance clashed with America's traditional capitalism and free enterprise. These beliefs dictated that every man should help himself and should be "free" of all external restraints on his economic activity. Protection for the weak in the form of government determination of work rules would upset the "natural law" of supply and demand existing between workers and employers. More than any other factor, the attacks by employers demanding a free labor market accounted for the death of the bureau.

After the Freedmen's Bureau was disbanded, much of the ground gained by blacks was lost through the connivance of Southern politicians and business leaders with Northern capital. A program of disenfranchisement and pauperization slowly eroded much of the progress blacks had made in education, business, and agriculture in the years immediately following the end of the war. In the midst of this new subjection of the black rose a leader of far-reaching magnitude, Booker T. Washington. In his most influential period, he was consulted whenever federal appointments were made in the South, whether they were to be filled with white or black people. He was the acknowledged leader of America's blacks from early in the 1880s until his death in 1915.

More than any black man of his time, Washington accepted the philosophy and projected the attitudes of individualism within the framework of capitalism. He was an outspoken apostle of the creed that only through individual achievement could the black race progress. He was forever pointing to the success stories of blacks in business as proof that economic success was indeed possible. His stories always emphasized the rewards of hard work, religion, and marital stability. One crucial feature of Washington's argument was that financial success was to be found in the trades or in agriculture. He believed that agriculture offered the quickest road to economic independence for blacks, for it provided the capital for other business investments.[11]

Washington believed that working with the soil would improve the black both morally and materially. He proposed that blacks work hard, save, and build capital to enter business. He encouraged the development of all-black towns, where blacks, rather than whites, would direct business and government. "This wealth which is the source of nearly all that we call capital, is often spoken of as unearned increment. The unearned increment usually goes to the man who gets on the ground first or to the man who knows best how to manage and direct his affairs. Under ordinary circumstances it goes to the white man. But in towns established and conducted by Negroes, it goes to the Negroes."[12] These towns would provide blacks with the base necessary to become equal with but separate from whites. Such ideas were well received by Southern whites and established Washington as a black man to be supported.

For the black to gain his independence, Washington suggested industrial education patterned on General S. C. Armstrong's program at Hampton Institute, the school he had attended. Armed with this normal and industrial education, common sense, and business ability, "any colored man can take a thousand dollars in cash and go into any Southern community and in five years be worth five thousand."[13]

In emphasizing the benefits of industrial education, Washington also stressed the advantages accruing to society, particularly white society, to whom he addressed most of his speeches. "Now these facts seem to show that manual training is almost as good a preventative of criminality as vaccination is of smallpox."[14] Washington wooed the Southern white almost religiously, and in so doing became the most powerful black men in the country and one of the most popular men in the South. In his autobiography, *Up From Slavery,* he indicated that blacks did not demand what whites most feared: social equality, the right to engage in higher intellectual pursuits, or a strong voice in politics. In 1884, before the National Education Association, he said:

A certain class of whites object to the general education of
the colored man on the ground that when he is educated he ceases

to do manual labor, and there is no avoiding the fact that much
aid is withheld from Negro education in the South by the states
on these grounds. Just here the great mission of Industrial Education, coupled with the mental, comes in. It kills two birds with
one stone; vis., it secures cooperation of the white and does the
best possible thing for the black man.[15]

Washington consistently advised his fellow blacks that the whites, particularly what he termed "the best white families," were to be emulated.
In this respect he reflected the ideology of the white, and specifically the
Southern white, leadership. During a period when blacks were being lynched
and disenfranchised, he never publicly alluded to these crimes. He embraced the mythology of Horatio Alger and the individualism of Theodore
Roosevelt. He also seemed to have been an apologist for slavery, as he used
the pro-slavery argument that slavery had been good for Africans because
it brought them civilization and Christianity:

> At the end of the period of slavery, about two hundred and fifty
> years, the Negro race as a whole had learned, as I have stated,
> to wear clothes, to live in a house, to work with a reasonable
> degree of regularity and system, and a few had learned to work
> with a high degree of skill. Not only this, the race had reached
> a point where from speaking scores of dialects, it had learned to
> speak intelligently the English language. It had a fair knowledge
> of American civilization and had changed from a pagan into a
> Christian Race.[16]

If Booker T. Washington was the period's most politically powerful black
man, W. E. B. DuBois was its most outstanding black intellectual. Poet,
writer, teacher, and sociologist, DuBois envisioned another road: "The
object of education was not to make men carpenters, but to make carpenters men."[17] Unlike Washington, DuBois did not advise hard work
and compromise. Instead he proclaimed that "the great lack of the Negro race and of nearly all the darker races today is *Energy,* self-assertive-
ness, the command and use of at least its more conspicuous powers."[18]
Although he was ambivalent about economic development through industrial education and entrepreneural business efforts, he clearly saw that
economic and cultural advancement under a system of capitalism required

college-trained leadership of a broader type. He believed that "the problem of education, then, among Negroes, must first of all deal with the talented tenth."[19] He remained firm on the need for the university-trained leader, even when, in his later years, he turned to communism. His concept of the talented tenth envisioned an educated black leadership that would assume positions as captains of industry and government.

At the same time, he recognized that since most black people were poor, their natural allies were other poor people; therefore, a greater public ownership of wealth would be in their best interests. DuBois's concept of economic development was much broader than Washington's concept of industrial education, work, and entrepreneural activity. DuBois always stressed the development of man in his total being, not just his economic self. He always feared that blacks would become more white than the whites and more capitalist than the capitalists: "What if the Negro people be wooed from a strife for righteousness, from a love of knowing, to regard dollars as the be-all and end-all of life?"[20]

Washington's attitude toward white discrimination and exploitation, his belief in manual or industrial education to the near exclusion of intellectual pursuits, along with his speech at the 1895 Atlanta Exposition, led to DuBois's public attack on Washington. In his 1895 Atlanta Exposition speech, which DuBois referred to as the Atlanta Compromise, Washington affirmed the concept of separation of the races. He stated that blacks and whites would work together for mutual benefits but remain separate in all things social. DuBois accused Washington of asking black people to give up political power, civil rights, and a higher education for their youth for the sake of industrial education, money, and conciliation of the South.[21]

Without actually saying it, DuBois seemed to sense that economic development as Washington viewed it would proletarianize blacks and that any advances blacks made would be at the expense of the great majority. He called big business "that science of human wants."[22] Finally, DuBois knew that the problems of poverty ran deeper than economic development, although he did recognize economics to be one element of the whole.

While DuBois opposed Washington for being an accommodationist, he opposed Marcus Garvey even more but on different grounds. He joined most of the influential black journalists of his day in calling Garvey either a scoundrel or a fool. DuBois rejected Garvey because he thought Garvey was taking money from thousands of black people for personal profit or for projects that were at best questionable. To DuBois, Garvey's program to establish a central nation for all black people was beyond reasonable expectation. Nevertheless, DuBois was not without some admiration for Garvey, perhaps even awe at his audacity. In *Black Moses* Edmund Cronon points out that DuBois admitted the feasibility of Garvey's plan: "What he is trying to say and do is this: American Negroes can, by accumulating and ministering their own capital, organize industry, join the black countries of the South Atlantic by commercial enterprise, and in this way ultimately redeem Africa as a fit and free home for black men. This is true. It is feasible, it is, in a sense, practical."[23]

Garvey, like Washington, was a staunch supporter of the capitalist system. He opposed socialism, even trade unionism, and he viewed capitalism as necessary to the progress of the world.[24] He differed with Washington only in his belief in black separatism.

Marcus Garvey started the Universal Negro Improvement Association in his home country of Jamaica and established the association in Harlem in 1917. Its main objectives were to build black economic enterprise, develop Africa as an independent world power, and unite all the black people of the world through an understanding of the dignity and beauty of blackness and developing race pride. Garvey believed that blacks could only be helped by blacks and that only through economic independence from the whites could they attain dignity and real freedom: "It takes the slave to interpret the spirit of his unfortunate brother; and so it takes the suffering Negro to interpret the spirit of his comrade."[25] Together with Washington he believed that blacks must become independent of white capital and operate their own businesses. They parted ways on the means of accomplishing black economic independence as well as on the final goal, which for Garvey was separation rather than pluralism.

Garvey's program was concerned not with the individual black, or even just American blacks, but with the race as a whole.

> The declared objectives of the UNIA were: To establish a universal confraternity among the race; to promote the spirit of pride and love: to reclaim the fallen; to administer to and assist the needy; to assist in civilizing the backward tribes of Africa; to assist in the development of independent Negro nations and communities; to establish a central nation for the race; to establish commissionaries of the world for the representation of all Negroes.[26]

Garvey's major economic effort centered on the Negro Factories Corporation and the Black Star Steamship Line. His plans for the Negro Factories Corporation were elaborate; they included a restaurant, a chain of cooperative grocery stores, a steam laundry, millinery shop, men's hat factory, publishing house, and a tailoring and dressmaking shop.[27] He also directed efforts to seek out business opportunities, interest black entrepreneurs in developing them, and offer executive and technical assistance, possibly also a loan of initial capital, to get them going.

The Black Star Line was originated to handle freight and passengers between Africa, the United States, Haiti, and other black or mostly black countries, with the idea of promoting black trade and economic well-being. Both the Black Star Line and the Negro Factories Corporation were designed to offer employment, management, and ownership opportunities for blacks, thereby creating black pride.

Garvey's first important attempt to create black pride was through the development of black-owned and -operated business enterprises. Millions of black people the world over joined the UNIA and invested their money and time in its development. Millions of others watched with mixed pride and doubt but always with excitement at the economic ups and downs of their enterprises.[28] The movement disintegrated after Garvey was sent to jail in 1925 for using the mails to defraud, but it has been carried on in different forms by former members. The Black Muslim movement of today, for example, is a lineal descendant. Another aspect of black economic control that reflects Garvey's influence is the "Don't Buy Where You Can't Work" campaign led by ad hoc organizations in almost every large city in the 1960s.

The views of Washington, DuBois, and Garvey are still in evidence among the present black leadership. The proponents of black capitalism for example, have borrowed ideas from both Washington and Garvey, notably Washington's pluralism and Garvey's concept of large-scale black enterprises. The advocates of black nationalism, on the other hand, see the problem of race as paramount, as Garvey did, while "the integrationists have been more willing to see the struggle of the black American in a class context,"[29] as DuBois did.

Some distinctions of the past are not so apparent today, however, as the black power advocates embrace accommodationist positions in their attempts to woo corporate America, and as integrationists embrace the credo of capitalism. Because of these compromises, America's response to poverty has been reflected in the black struggle for economic parity. That struggle has been made necessary by the exigencies of capitalism.

While Washington, DuBois, and Garvey sought ways of helping their race to cope in a society based on capitalist competition and openly dedicated to racism, the nation's leadership busied itself with increasing opportunities for big business. In the 1920s the country was in the midst of an economic boom, while most blacks and the other poor were mostly ignored. According to the dominant view, poverty was a reflection of the person's own failure; hence, those who were poor by and large deserved their lot.

Responsibility for the care of the poor in the United States was a local matter. Public responsibility generally included only widows, orphans, the aged, and the disabled. The able-bodied were expected to care for themselves and their families. Most of those in control endorsed a concept of economic individualism. Because of the widespread acceptance of the doctrine of self-help through work and the limitation of welfare to local government, only local relief arrangements were available when the depression of the 1930s hit full force.[30]

Herbert Hoover reflected the attitude of the nation's business leaders on federal welfare when, during his first campaign for the presidency, he stated that "the true growth of the nation is the growth of character in its citizens. The spread of government destroys initiative and thus destroys character. Character is made in the community as well as in the individual by assuming responsibilities not by escaping from them."[31] His later emphasis on the cooperation of big business and other leadership was prefigured during this first campaign: "Without intrusion the government can sometimes give leadership and serve to bring together divergent elements and secure cooperation in developing ideas, measures, and institutions. This is a reinforcement of our individualism."[32] Thus, Hoover plainly favored self-help and advocated that the government encourage cooperative efforts in the private sector.

Hoover's campaign speeches were faithful to America's tradition of individualism and free enterprise. Institutions, he said, should be under the local control of citizens who knew their own needs. He emphasized self-help as the mainspring of responsible citizenship.

Hoover was elected in 1928 and the depression began a year later. Hoover responded to the continued increase in unemployment by insisting that federal aid only be used as a supplement to the timid state and local efforts. He took the lead in encouraging the establishment of voluntary cooperative actions by such groups as the National Business Survey Conference, the National Credit Corporation, the President's Emergency Committee for Employment, and the President's Organization of Unemployment Relief. In addition, these institutions looked to others for support, such as the national trade associations, the National Association of Community Chests, the United States Chamber of Commerce, bank associations, private charity organizations and city, county, and state governments.

Hoover's program of voluntary cooperative action by corporations, business leaders, and the people in general was consistently unsuccessful.[33] Even the private charities did not accept a government role as appropriate. The American Red Cross, for example, rejected $25 million appropriated by Congress for the relief of drought sufferers in 1931. President Hoover applauded the Red Cross action, stating that "a voluntary deed by a man impressed with the sense of responsibility and brotherhood of man is infinitely more precious than a thousandfold poured from the treasury under compulsion of the law."[34] So, for Hoover, an individual or local act of charity had higher moral value than assistance from government.

Thus, only local relief arrangements were made to deal with the national emergency created by continued business failure and unemployment. These local efforts became increasingly inoperative in the face of massive unemployment and the concomitant social problems. Newspapers began to encourage people to find odd jobs for the unemployed, and cities initiated make-a-job campaigns and household helper schemes. Philadelphia formed a committee to organize street selling of fruits, and as stated earlier, Chickasha, Oklahoma, allowed the unemployed to scrape food left on restaurant plates into containers, on condition that they chop wood donated by farmers.[35] In 1933, unemployment climbed to a high of 15 million— one of every three in the total work force. Even so, Hoover persisted in his view that the economy was merely experiencing a healthful deflation of unnatural speculative values and that business would soon be resumed on a sound basis.

By March 1933, when Franklin Delano Roosevelt took office as president, the country and the world was in the midst of one of its worst depressions. Many banks had been forced to close, and Roosevelt called a bank holiday to forstall total collapse. He moved immediately to involve the federal government in the first broadbased relief program ever created and the only program of federal relief since the Freedmen's Bureau. During his famous hundred days, he signed into law the Emergency Banking Act, Economy Act, Civilian Conservation Corporation, Agriculture Adjustment Act, Federal Emergency Relief Act, Truth-in-Securities Act, Home Owners Loan Act, Glass-Steagall Banking Act, Farm Credit Act, Railroad Coordination Act, and National Industrial Recovery Act. During this period, the gold standard was abandoned.[36] All of these actions were taken in a country where the politically dominant groups had by and large been committed to noninterference by the federal government and had championed the ideology of individualism. These changes were enacted so quickly that, at least in the beginning, even the business leaders applauded Roosevelt. Businessmen soon returned to the familiar position that relief should be a local responsibility, once "the light at the end of the tunnel"[37] was glimpsed.

While it is impossible to completely separate the results of any one of the emergency acts of 1933 from any of the others, for our purposes one important approach, that of the National Industrial Recovery Act (NRA), will be singled out and reviewed briefly. More completely than any other, this act embraces the philosophy upon which welfare has been traditionally based: self-help and work. Although the Federal Emergency Relief Act probably reached as many or more unemployed people with an expenditure of over $3 billion from 1933 to its termination in 1935, and although the still-existing Tennessee Valley Authority has had a longer legal lifetime, the NRA had the most profound and lasting effect on the nation's institutions. The NRA directly affected the relationship of labor to business and the position of each within the larger society.

The NRA attempted to facilitate economic recovery by spreading available work through a reduction of the number of working hours per man per week. In a speech on July 5, 1933, Donald R. Richberg, general counsel of the NRA, said that "the objectives of the National Industrial Recovery Act are well understood and universally approved. They are: to put more people to work; to give them more buying power; to insure just rewards for both capital and labor in sound business enterprise, by eliminating unfair competition."[38] It was, in fact, a bold attempt at federal intervention by putting more money into the hands of consumers to purchase more products, which in turn was to produce more demand for equipment and raw materials and ultimately expand production, trade, and the number of necessary workers. Benefits were to be added to benefits until the progression to economic recovery was well established.

One major section of the NRA legislation established a fund of $3.3 billion for a two-year period for the financing of public works. These federal government funds were matched by state moneys and were intended to finance federal buildings, hospitals, schools, new roads, and the like and at the same time provide employment. Thousands of people across the country found employment through the resulting Works Project Administration (WPA).

As important as WPA was in halting unemployment, the NRA had even greater implications for the role of the federal government. It attempted to provide economic development by forcing the major components, capital and labor, into cooperative action for the national benefit. The federal government had at last intervened—no matter what the effect or motivation— on behalf of the worker, children, and the poor generally. In contrast to his predecessor's voluntary cooperation of business, Roosevelt established enforced cooperation. At the same time, he assisted in the creation of unions, set the tone for legislation on child labor, minimum wages, fair labor practices, and many other rights we now take for granted.

Neither the NRA nor any of the other programs of the "one hundred days" eliminated poverty in the United States. Indeed, such was not the intent of the programs. After all, Roosevelt was responding not to poverty but to crisis business conditions and the widespread discontent of labor. His major concerns were to direct business back on a profitable path and to get organized labor back on the job and under control. At the same time, he used the rhetoric of self-help and full employment to provide the illusion that his programs were designed to help the poor. The fact is that the chronic unemployed, which included most black people, remained unemployed until World War II when they enlisted in the service or were hired to replace someone who had gone into the service.

From the time of the Acts of Enclosure and the early Industrial Revolution in England, the poor have been exploited. Society in large part has accepted the premise that the poor themselves are responsible for their poverty and thus deserving of the harshness of their lives.

As a result, those who control society have hesitated, even opposed, adopting programs designed to bring about direct relief, free of humiliation and punishment to the recipients. The most humane approach has always embraced self-help programs or programs designed to change the character of the poor through education. Charity, or more properly philanthropy, has been concerned more with justifying wealth than correcting poverty.

The foregoing perspective attempts to focus on some of the responses to poverty that have lineal ties with the community economic development movement. The emphasis on black approaches to economic survival results from both the black's traditional economic position and the black leadership's acceptance of capitalism with its associated concepts of self-help and individualism. It is through this historical tradition that we arrive at today's community economic development corporation.

NOTES

1. Samuel Mencher, *Poor Law to Poverty Program* (Pittsburgh, Penn.: Pittsburgh University Press, 1967), p. 242.

2. See William C. Heffner, *Poor Laws—Pennsylvania* (Cleona, Penn.: Holzapful Publishing Co., 1913).

3. Robert H. Bremner, *American Philanthropy* (Chicago: University of Chicago Press, 1960), p. 24.

4. Jerome Bennett, Jr., *Before the Mayflower: A History of the Negro in America* (Chicago: Johnson Publishing Co., Inc., 1966), pp. 152-153.

5. William H. Pease and Jane H. Pease, *Black Utopia: Negro Communal Experiments in America* (Madison: The State Historical Society of Wisconsin, 1963), p. 13.

6. Ibid., p. 19.

7. Ibid., p. 21.

8. Ibid., p. 30.

9. Bennett, op. cit., p. 187.

10. George R. Bentley, *A History of the Freedmen's Bureau* (New York: Octagon Books, 1970), p. 34.

11. Booker T. Washington, *The Negro in Business* (New York: AMS Press, 1971), p. 28.

12. Ibid., pp. 68-69.

13. Victoria Earl Mathew, ed., *Black Belt Diamonds: Gems from the Speeches, Addresses, and Talks to Students of Booker T. Washington* (New York: Negro University Press, 1969), p. 16.

14. Louis R. Harlan and John W. Blessingame, eds., *The Booker T. Washington Papers,* Vol. 1 (Chicago: University of Illinois Press, 1972), p. 64.

15. Ibid., p. 46.

16. Booker T. Washington and W. E. B. DuBois, *The Negro in the*

South (New York: Citadel Press, 1970), pp. 25-26.

17. Herbert Aptheker, ed., *The Education of Black People: Ten Critiques, 1906-1960, By W. E. B. DuBois* (Amherst: University of Massachusetts Press, 1973), p. 64.

18. Ibid., p. 7.

19. Rayford W. Logan, ed., *W. E. B. DuBois: A Profile* (New York: Hill and Wang, 1971), p. 74.

20. W. E. B. DuBois, *The Souls of Black Folk* (Greenwich, Conn.: Fawcett Publications, 1961), p. 48.

21. Ibid., p. 48.

22. W. E. B. DuBois, *Darkwater* (New York: Schocken Books, 1969), p. 119.

23. Edmund David Cronon, *Black Moses* (Madison: University of Wisconsin Press, 1969), p. 209.

24. William L. Henderson and Larry Ledebur, *Economic Disparity: Problems and Strategies for Black America* (New York: Free Press, 1970), p. 41.

25. A. J. Garvey, ed., *The Philosophy and Opinion of Marcus Garvey* (New York: Universal Publishing House, 1923), p. 74.

26. Amy Jacques Garvey, *Garvey and Garveyism* (London: Collier-Macmillan, Ltd., 1963), Intro. XII.

27. See Elton C. Fox, *Garvey* (New York: Dodd, Mead and Co., 1972), p. 60.

28. Joanne Grant, ed., *Black Protest* (Greenwich, Conn.: Fawcett Publications, 1970), p. 179.

29. Theodore G. Vincent, *Black Power and the Garvey Movement* (Berkeley, Calif.: Ramparts Press, 1971), pp. 51-52.

30. Frances Fox Piven and Richard A. Cloward, *Regulating the Poor: The Functions of Public Welfare* (New York: Random House, 1971), pp. 46-48.

31. Herbert Hoover, *The New Day, Campaign Speeches of Herbert Hoover, 1928* (Stanford, Calif.: Stanford University Press, 1928), p. 17.

32. Ibid., p. 19.

33. Albert V. Romasco, *The Poverty of Abundance* (New York: Oxford University Press, 1965), pp. 181-182.

34. Bremmer, p. 145.

35. Piven and Cloward, op. cit., p. 49.

36. Ibid., p. 71.

37. A saying made famous during the depression, along with "recovery is right around the corner."

38. Charles L. Dearing, et al., *The ABC of the NRA* (Washington, D.C.: The Brookings Institution, 1934), p. 32.

2

THE COMMUNITY DEVELOPMENT CORPORATION CONCEPT

The CDC was born out of the centuries' long struggle for civil rights, the urban riots of the 1960s, the Ford Foundation's Grey Area program[1] and the federal government's Community Action Agency (CAA) program.[2] Its purpose was clearly defined in Title VII of the Community Economic Development Amendment to the Economic Opportunity Act of 1964, which stated that the CDCs were intended: "to encourage the development of special programs by which the residents of urban and rural low-income areas may through self-help and mobilization of the community at large with appropriate Federal assistance, improve the quality of their economic and social participation in community life in such a way as to contribute to the elimination of poverty and the establishment of permanent economic and social benefits.[3] The objective, as stated by the National Advisory Council on Economic Development, is "to break the cycle of poverty in low-income communities by arresting tendencies toward dependency, chronic unemployment, and community deterioration."[4]

The CDC is thus meant to be a partnership between the community, government, and the private business sector.[5] The community is to provide the manpower, overall direction, and framework within which the CDC functions and is to be the source of the human and physical resources of the CDC. The government is to be the major source of funding, provide some technical assistance and direction, preferential consideration on government contracts, and support the CDC in its development goals. The private sector is to participate through the membership of corporate executives on the CDC board and subsidiary boards, by providing technical assistance, cooperating in joint ventures with the CDC, and assisting the CDC in training staff and management personnel. Private corporations are also to give special marketing advantages to the CDC and provide financial grants and loans.

To accomplish the objective, a variety of strategies are used, such as the acquisition of existing businesses, the development of new businesses, investment in the physical assets of the community, assistance through loans and technical service to community entrepreneurs, and participation with private sector interests in joint ventures. Even more important to the accomplishment of the objective is the realization of the concept of community control.

The early OEO/CDC staff thought that community control was necessary for the proper functioning of the CDC. They believed that without it people outside the community would define problems, as a result of which the interaction necessary for developing equality with the greater society would be impossible. With community members functioning as board members, senior staff members, secretaries, block workers, entrepreneurs, and managers, and with these community members negotiating with like members of corporations outside the community, the community self-image would become positive. Moreover, it was argued that this broad participation would increase community skills. Some CDC advocates also maintain that this participation advances the cause of integration, since it provides for the mutual respect and parity between the races necessary for true integration. Therefore, community control becomes the vehicle for greater understanding between the races by giving blacks the opportunity for meeting white counterparts as equals in a business environment. The CDC concept also implies an attempt to alter the dependent relationship to external agencies that has been characteristic for many community residents.

CDC advocates believe that through community control the community rather than the individual becomes the client and recipient of benefits. This focus on the community enables the individual to grow through self-achievement, and it removes the stigma of paternalism associated with programs designed specifically for the individual. The individual participates in making decisions that can improve not only the community but, as a direct consequence, his own environment and life chances as well. The community as client is a major factor in the community control concept.

Another major thesis underlying the CDC concept holds that community members who become managers, directors of boards, and presidents of businesses learn new skills and become participants rather than observers of the system. Through participation they are presumed to learn about the system and therefore become better able to cope with its complexities. By negotiating a loan, closing a real estate contract, or assisting in an audit of a subsidiary, residents shed their feelings of inadequacy and helplessness.

Community development evolved from the notion that the community should have greater control over community activities and assets. In poor communities, most businesses and property are owned by people outside the community; hence, the benefits derived from this ownership also accrue to these outsiders. A change to local ownership is thought to enable the community to develop a self-sustaining process of economic development. The business, then, directly benefits the community, and the profits from the business are retained by the community for reinvestment.

According to the CDC rationale, initiating a new business in the community produces benefits similar to those created by acquiring an existing business. In addition, it holds that the new business provides jobs that did not exist before. Generally, a new business carries a greater risk, however, since the CDC will only purchase profitable ongoing businesses. The CDC does aid new businesses in their difficult early stages and until they attain some measure of stability and profitability. Moreover, the risk involved in the new venture is reduced because it is entered into jointly with an established corporation. In such an arrangement, the established corporation provides a marketing umbrella for the new venture and supplies technical assistance in the form of a management component. The management component usually consists of a one-to-one relationship of community and technical assistance personnel in all major management areas and is continued until the community managers are fully capable of accepting management responsibility. The joint venture relationship is only continued until the new business can stand alone, at which time the established corporation divests its ownership shares through a sale to the community.

The CDC can also stabilize and strengthen existing community-owned businesses. The resident entrepreneur brings his experiences and skills, as well as some financial commitment, to the new venture, and the CDC provides seed capital and technical assistance. The CDC also assists in marketing through its associations in the larger economic community.

The development of new businesses is important to the CDC, but of equal importance is physical development, which includes the building of new homes, construction of new buildings to house businesses and community facilities, renovation of older homes and office buildings, and development of apartment complexes and shopping centers. Physical development will improve the environment, create community amenities, develop locations for new businesses, and increase employment. Whenever possible, such projects utilize community contractors and workers. In cases where competent community contractors cannot be found, the contractor employed is frequently required to hire a specific number of community people who are trained on the job.

With successful business and physical development, profits are provided for reinvestment in the community. Through community control, the residents themselves make the decisions as to how profits are to be reinvested. These profits can be placed in socially beneficial projects such as day care centers, centers for the elderly, health centers, and head-start programs, or they can be used to start new businesses. Regardless of what choice is made, of major importance to the CDC is the fact that the community, and not people outside the community, makes the final decision.

An additional factor relating to community control is the political influence resulting from community organization and consensual action. A greater portion of the city's services and improved assistance from City Hall is assumed to become more possible when a unified front is presented. The existence of a representative organization with a significant black vote potential makes every level of government more receptive to the community.

As important as community control is, the CDC effort cannot be successful without the participation of the external private business sector and government. As mentioned earlier, the private sector takes part through joint venture efforts and by providing marketing advantages to CDC enterprises. In addition, CDC planners envisioned the direct involvement of representatives of major outside business interests in the management of both the CDC and CDC subsidiary efforts. This type of participation is expected also to lead these business representatives to take a larger interest in community problems through a better understanding of the community resulting from direct exposure to the ghetto and the people living there.

Representatives of the private sector are intended to serve on the CDC board of directors and on the boards of directors of the subsidiary corporations. The CDC board appointments are filled by managers and officers of large corporations, when possible, and by banking representatives, lawyers, and CPAs. Subsidiary appointments are filled by business and technical representatives familiar with the problems of the subsidiary corporation. In either case, they are expected to become links to the larger society and advocates for the CDC programs, and to use their influence to obtain loans, grants, and other technical assistance. In the case of community businesses that sell products, these links would be of particular importance because these individuals would be able to intervene with purchasing people to secure markets for CDC products. In addition, they would add substance to the CDC board and credibility to CDC activities.

Representatives of the private sector who serve on subsidiary boards are expected to offer a specialized skill related to the needs of the particular subsidiary. For example, a CDC chemical company might have a chemical engineer from a large corporation on its board, or a CDC manufacturer an industrial engineer. Accountants and lawyers are always in demand, for every company needs their assistance.

Technical assistance is most important to CDC efforts in areas demanding skills beyond those available at the staff level or in the community. Corporations can provide specialized individuals, or even teams, to work with community ventures until the new management becomes sufficiently competent to manage on its own. This type of participation satisfies the training need and at the same time develops rapport between the community and corporations. As mentioned earlier, it is also thought to promote integration of the races.

Board participation and technical assistance could lead to market advantages for the CDC and CDC subsidiaries. If board members from the private sector are chosen carefully, and if those providing technical assistance are from related industries, there might be opportunities to sell to their companies. If the subsidiary and private sector corporations are in the same or related businesses, there might also be subcontract possibilities. The private sector can also support the CDC by grants or loans. Placing CDC venture funds in a bank encourages preferential loan terms and can perhaps break the "red lining," or outlining of areas where groups are considered loan risks, that makes it difficult for inner-city businesses to get loans. Most grants emanate from foundations and can be obtained for specific categories through proposals. Some grants are made through the efforts of a company officer, as a matter of corporate responsibility. The CDC concept assumed that businesses would be anxious to become involved because of their sense of corporate responsibility.

Corporations also benefit from actions motivated by social conscience. Since most of these acts are publicized, their public relations value often far outstrips their cost to the corporation. Subliminal advertising is often cloaked in a socially beneficial act. For example, Mobil Oil placed an advertisement in the January 23, 1975, issue of the *New York Times,* extolling the benefits potentially available to society through CDC efforts and encouraging other corporations to become involved. Significantly, the ad was placed during the period when the oil industry was receiving intense criticism. Thus, the message was clear: Mobil was not a crook! As is evident, even self-serving aspects of the private sector can be of advantage to CDCs.

The CDC has a mandate to improve the quality of life of the community residents through an economic development program that opens up new opportunities for employment, development of new skills, ownership of property, and accumulation of capital for community improvement. Through acquiring existing businesses owned by outside interests, creating new enterprises, and developing the community's physical assets, the CDC is to accomplish its goals of community development. The following chapters attempt to show whether the CDCs' concepts have become reality.

NOTES

1. An experiment by the Ford Foundation in the 1960s to provide funding for self-help community programs, later designated community development corporations.

part 2

A CASE STUDY: UNION SARAH ECONOMIC DEVELOPMENT CORPORATION

INTRODUCTION

As is true of most of the urban areas served by CDCs, the Union Sarah Community Economic Development Corporation (USEDC) area is a black ghetto characterized by large-scale poverty. It was defined as a discrete geographic area in 1968, with the creation of the Union Sarah Community Corporation (USCC), a branch of the St. Louis Community Action Agency (the Human Development Corporation). For administrative purposes, boundaries were designated for the various CAA branches. Union and Sarah are names of streets that form the east-west boundaries of the area.

Originally, the area was an upper middle-class suburban residential area. The homes were spacious single-family dwellings on large lots, some of them of estate size. Between 1910 and 1925, most of the large lots were broken up for expanded housing construction, but the area remained primarily a white upper middle-class community. To understand the area's transformation into a black, lower income community, we need to consider the racial and economic changes that have reshaped the entire city.

In 1860, the black population of St. Louis numbered only 27,000, or about 6 percent of the total population. It remained relatively small until about 1920, a time when no single large black ghetto existed in the city. The black population increased to 93,580, or 11.4 percent in 1930, 18 percent in 1950, 30 percent in 1960, and over 42 percent in 1970.[1]

Along with the increased black population each decade after 1920 saw shifts in population distribution. Through the 1920s and 1930s, a large black ghetto arose in an area known as Mill Creek, situated to the east of Union Sarah, close to the business district. At this same time, the area in and around Union Sarah began to be populated by black servants, teachers, ministers, and professionals. In the late 1930s and the 1940s, increased numbers of blacks migrated to St. Louis from the South in order to get war industry employment, and Union Sarah's black population rose to over 50 percent.

Two major events during the 1950s brought the black population of Union Sarah over the 97 percent mark. Between 1950 and 1960, St. Louis ranked first among the nation's cities in population loss. The total population declined by 12 percent, but the black population increased 40 percent in the same period.[2] In addition, the construction of the Mill Creek urban renewal project caused a great displacement of blacks, bringing a large number of blacks north and west. Many moved from what had been the black ghetto in the heart of the city into the Union Sarah area. The population of Union Sarah rose to 42,000 in 1960.

With the overcrowding of Union Sarah, most housing units were converted to multi-family dwellings. Even so, a sizable population of black middle-class families remained; they still live in well-maintained properties and are active in the community. A larger proportion of the area housing, however, is in an extreme state of decay and can be described, at best, as substandard.

The area is mostly residential, with some light industrial and commercial enterprises located on the major arteries. Heavy industrial efforts are not attracted to the area, as there are no rail facilities. The major arteries have always been primarily commercial. All have shopping areas within the Union Sarah boundaries. One shopping area contains small clothing and household furnishings stores, small restaurants, bars, pawnshops, a bank, office buildings, and the area post office. In the past, ownership of the businesses was almost completely white, but in the last fifteen years many of these businesses have left the area and blacks have taken over their shop locations. Most of the black businesses are small and tenuous; the larger enterprises, e.g., the bank, pawnshops, five and dime, and appliance store, are still white-owned and operated. At another location, the major businesses are a Sears store, a home loan and savings bank, and two supermarkets. Several clothing shops and a furniture store are also located in this block. Again, all of these were owned by whites until very recently, when a Kroger supermarket closed. As will be discussed later, this location was taken over by USEDC and operated as the Union Sarah Community IGA.

On all of these major arteries, commercial businesses and light industry were dominant and mostly white-owned. In the past twenty years, many of the larger concerns have either gone out of business or moved. Their locations were not taken over by new owners because in many cases they were obsolete; as a result, the vacant buildings contribute to the overall deterioration of the area.

As of the 1970 census, approximately 32,000 people were living in Union Sarah, a decline of 10,000 persons since the 1960 census. The reason for this large decrease is that the young upward mobile blacks and almost all the remaining whites have moved away. Approximately 97 percent of Union Sarah is now black, with an equal number above and below the age of twenty-five. The income level indicates a high degree of unemployment and underemployment, with 3,298 of 6,984 families having incomes below or within the range of poverty, as defined by 1970 census guidelines. Table 1 provides income data for the Union Sarah area, while

Table 1

FAMILY INCOME, 1970

Total families	6,984
Below $6,000	3,298
$6,000-$6,999	592
$7,000-$7,999	520
$8,000-$8,999	508
$9,000 and above	2,066

Table 2 delineates population by age and sex. Both tables were compiled from the 1970 Census of Population and Housing.

Table 2

AGE DISTRIBUTION OF USEDC POPULATION, BY SEX

Males	
14 and below	4,462
15-18	1,182
19-24	1,392
25-34	1,664
35-44	1,548
45 and above	5,187

Females	
14 and below	4,531
15-18	1,301
19-24	1,849
25-34	1,780
35-44	1,875
45 and above	6,897

The Union Sarah Economic Development Corporation was established by the Union Sarah Community Corporation, with the assistance of the Neighborhood Advisory Council of the Union Sarah area and the Human Development Corporation, which is the St. Louis Community Action Program. The relationships between these organizations are complex, with many overlapping functions and responsibilities, and they have changed over the years.

The Neighborhood Advisory Council (NAC) began in 1966 as the acting board of directors guiding the activities of the community center established by the Human Development Corporation (HDC). Each center in the city, named Gateway Centers by HDC, had a Neighborhood Advisory Council made up of residents. In 1968, with the establishment of community corporations at many of the center sites and a move toward decentralization by HDC, many NACs were replaced by community corporation boards. Some NACs still function, despite questions as to their legality. Some active residents consider them ad hoc organizations.

USCC, the parent corporation and majority stockholder of USEDC, was organized in March 1968 as a nonprofit community corporation and arm of HDC. It was through the efforts of USCC, HDC, and NAC that USEDC came into being. Table 3 delineates the relationships of other organizations to USEDC, including that of OEO. These relationships have since changed, as reflected in Table 4.

The experiences of those involved in USCC led to greater interest in the need to go beyond merely improved community services. Some community activists embraced the idea that the community needed to work to rebuild its economic structure and to stimulate the kind of economic activity that, it was hoped, would create more jobs, help local business, and contribute to the general well-being of the area. These sentiments led to interest in new federal legislation that empowered OEO to provide funds for local economic development corporations.

On January 14, 1969, a little less than a year after USCC was inaugurated, a meeting was held at USCC to discuss the possibility of putting together a proposal for Title 1-D funds and organizing an economic development corporation.[3] The proposal was assembled and submitted in a great rush, in order to meet the OEO submittal date for that grant period. With less than a month to put the package together, it was decided to make the attempt and HDC staff members gave assurances of their support and assistance. A meeting was planned for January 17, when the question would be placed before a representative group from the community.

The meeting on January 17 was attended by three staff members from USCC, three staff members from HDC, five local businessmen, one bank vice-president, three members of NAC, two USCC board members, a prominent local politician, and representatives from the Tandy Area Council, Mid-City Community Congress, CORE, ACTION, the West St. Louis Community Center, and the St. Louis Municipal Business Development Commission. This grouping was certainly a broad-based representation of the community organizations and business and city agencies, but was hardly representative of the area poor. Nevertheless, the desirability of establishing an economic development corporation as an approach to alleviating area poverty was supported unanimously; a steering committee was set up; plans were made to contact local corporations and representatives of

Table 3

ORGANIZATIONAL RELATIONSHIP, 1969

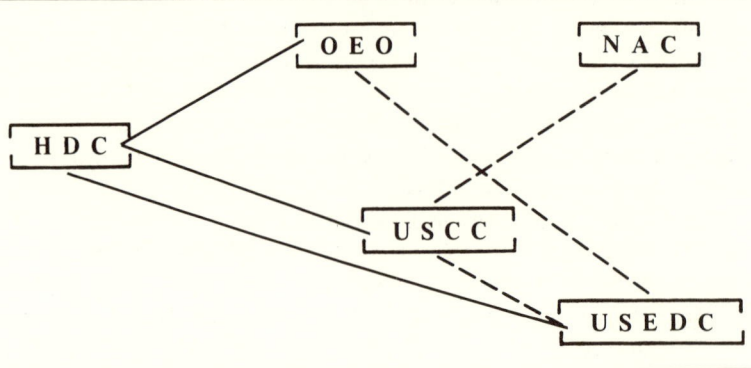

Table 4

ORGANIZATIONAL RELATIONSHIP, 1975

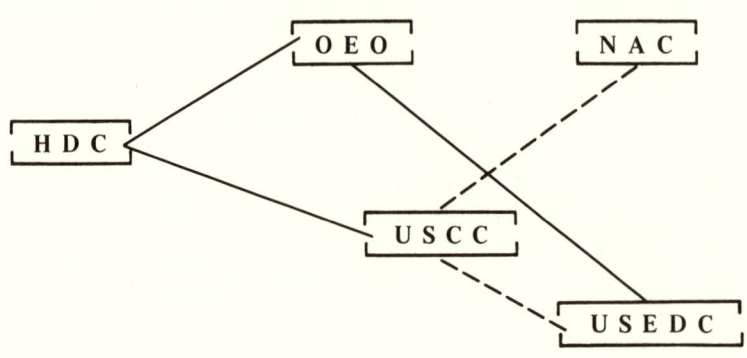

KEY TO CHARTS:

Direct Reporting ─────────────

Informational or Functional Reporting ─ ─ ─ ─ ─ ─ ─ ─ ─

federal, state, and local government agencies for support; and several members of the group were assigned as a committee to travel to Cleveland, Ohio, to observe the operation of the Hough Area Development Corporation, an already established CDC.

OEO extended the deadline, and the proposal, referred to as Special Impact Program One (SIP 1), was submitted on April 2. During the three months from January to April, a board of directors was chosen, a beginning staff selected, and suggestions and studies for an aluminum extrusion plant, shopping center, automobile service center, casket manufacturing company, insurance company, dry cleaning plant, and several more enterprises were made and reviewed by various committees. The first board of directors meeting was held on March 26, formal approval for the program was given by OEO on May 7, and the Certificate of Incorporation in the state of Missouri was issued on June 13, 1969. The Union Sarah Economic Development Corporation had become a reality.

NOTES

1. U.S. Bureau of the Census, Census of the United States, St. Louis Missouri Abstracts, as cited in Gary Allen Tobin, "The St. Louis School Crisis: Population Shifts and Voting Patterns" (St. Louis: Washington University Department of History, June 1970).

2. Ibid., p. 25.

3. Title 1-D funds are so called because the amendment to the 1964 Office of Economic Development legislation creating the community development corporation was designated the 1-D Amendment.

3
A BRIEF HISTORY OF USEDC

USEDC, organized as a "for profit" corporation under the laws of the state of Missouri, functions under the guidance of a twenty-nine-member board of directors. Control of the board is held by the community corporation within which 51 percent of the stock is vested. The community corporation, USCC, is a "not-for-profit" corporation and was the sponsor for the original OEO grant. The members of the USCC board of directors are elected by the residents of the Union Sarah community. All residents sixteen years and older are permitted to vote for the board members. USEDC board members are elected at the USEDC annual stockholders' meeting, with the provision that at least 51 percent, or fifteen, must be members of the USCC board.

Originally, HDC acted as the "grantee" of the OEO grant and as such was the conduit for funds from OEO to USEDC. HDC also functioned in a monitoring role to USEDC. However, both OEO and USEDC believed that HDC involvement added only another layer of bureaucracy; thus HDC was removed from any direct involvement, acting thereafter only as an advocate and associate agency. USEDC is presently funded directly by OEO, and HDC monitoring activities have ceased.

The president, who is the chief executive officer of the corporation, reports to the board of directors. The staff totals twelve and is divided into three departments: Administrative, Real Estate, and Venture Formation and Management. All department heads report to the president.

The USCC board of directors determines the desirability of any venture activity recommended by the staff, while the USEDC board of directors determines the feasibility of any proposal placed before it for review. In this way, the two boards complement one another, and the major decision as to whether a project is wanted by the community is left with USCC. Because the feasibility of the project is a decision of the USEDC board, its board membership is dominated by business interests.

In addition to the board and staff functions, there are working committees, the members of which are drawn from both board and staff personnel. The major committees are the Fiscal Committee, charged with reviewing budgets and performance against budgets of USEDC and subsidiary performance as well; the Manufacturing Committee, responsible for passing on the initial feasibility of new projects; and the Personnel Committee, responsible for the initial review of recommended new employees, the development of personnel procedures and policy, and acting as a grievance committee when needed. The board and senior staff also participate on the boards of directors of all subsidiary companies and serve on any committees established as part of those responsibilities.

The subsidiary corporations have boards of directors, at least 51 percent of which are made up of the board of USEDC; the remaining members are drawn from the business community. Every attempt is made to include on these boards people with either the skills or professional connections to assist the corporations in their successful operation.

It is always difficult to differentiate between goals and objectives. For our purposes the term *goal* will be used to designate the final desired results, and the term *objective* will designate a specific desired achievement developed to move toward the goal. For example, a goal might be to expand employment for area residents. An objective for reaching that goal might be to establish a manufacturing plant.

The goals of USEDC have remained constant from its inception and have coincided closely with those of the national CDC movement. These goals are to improve the quality of life for the poor people of the Union Sarah area by creating jobs for residents; by physical development of the area to include much-needed new and rehabilitated housing; by providing community control of community resources through the acquisition of existing businesses now owned by outside sources; by creating new business in the community; and by providing upward mobility opportunities for residents through their participation in the decision-making processes, through which they are to gain self-confidence and effect changes in their self-image.

The specific objectives for achieving the goals have changed over time. As attempts to implement one set of objectives were frustrated, a new set had to be formulated. Milestone charts and planning narratives outlining objectives were supposed to be developed through board participation and then used by OEO as a measure of progress. The objectives for the original proposal were:

1. To establish and maintain manufacturing enterprises of the size that could have impact on the area in terms of resident employment, managerial training and positions, community control, and profit returning to the community.

2. To establish a contractors' revolving fund and training program through a contractors' association in conjunction with a housing program to upgrade existing residential and commercial structures in the area.

3. To develop a shopping complex to serve the basic Union Sarah impact area as well as the total community. This shopping complex would be resident-owned and located within the jurisdictional boundaries of the USDC as set forth in this document.

4. To provide, through this development corporation, a seed fund wherein moneys would be available for the expansion of the existing resident-owned businesses and the establishment of new ones that the corporation believed useful and needed.

5. To develop and train personnel with which to staff this corporation and other business enterprises established under its jurisdiction.

6. To participate in and have some control over business operations within the target area, thereby assuring resident community control of this area's economic future for its citizenry.

7. To foster a policy that seeks to interest major companies in the possibilities of establishing subsidiary or branch operations within the Union Sarah area.

8. To coordinate the efforts of other participating community organizations in the economic area, thus providing a highly unified effort. The residents of the area view that unity as a prime concern in the successful implementation of the authorized program.

9. To demonstrate that community organization and economic development can be successfully linked for the improvement of the general community.

10. To develop a self-sustaining operation.[1]

The projected measurable results for the original proposal were:

1. Four hundred jobs for residents ranging from the unskilled to managerial level.

2. Ownership and interest in community economic development projects capitalized at $4 million.

3. Sale of $48,000 of stock.

4. Breakeven point on investments in two years—a small profit in five years.

5. Improvement of fifty houses and doubling of work handled by the contractors.[2]

The basic strategy for accomplishing the objectives of the program, and indeed for approaching the measurable projected results, was to coalesce all of the resources of greater St. Louis behind projects that were labor intensive. Another part of the strategy was to attract business and industry to the area by encouraging them to participate in joint ventures with the community, or to locate plants in the area that would benefit through leasing community property or facilities on better than market terms. Cooperating firms could also benefit through their participation in government programs that offered on-the-job training grants, zoning relief from

the city, and possible tax benefits from the Missouri blighting legislation.
USEDC also hoped for participation from lending institutions, through
whom they hoped to leverage their $900,000 grant from OEO by a margin
of 4 to 1 by obtaining guaranteed loans.

Priorities based on the stated strategy were established in the proposal.
As might be expected, manufacturing, which was expected to be the most
labor intensive, was the first and highest priority item. A large manufacturing effort would eliminate much of the unemployment in the area and
provide the kind of return on investment necessary to carry on the social
programs the area so desperately needed. In accordance with the early
advocates of the 1-D legislation, those developing the proposal envisioned
community people as plant managers, accountants, field salesmen, engineers,
and a major portion of the workforce. The salary levels that these positions
commanded would give the community members self-assurance and also
provide them with incomes that would allow them to spend more money
in community stores. Many of the people involved in the original proposal
and subsequent efforts were tradesmen from the area. Community development would both increase their profits and create a healthy business community.

Of over fifteen manufacturing projects considered, two were selected
as most feasible: Aero-Tech Industries, a dry lubricant coating process;
and an aluminum extrusion plant. These two projects seemed to offer
the greatest employment and expansion possibilities. And, too, since the
products from these industries could be used by a wide variety of businesses,
they would open up the potential for wide private sector involvement in
the newly formed CDC. It was expected that corporations, particularly
local St. Louis corporations, would offer preferential marketing opportunities to the CDC. Although the framers of USEDC were unanimous in their
enthusiasm for these projects, neither proved viable because their investment requirements were beyond USEDC capabilities. USEDC did not
become involved in a manufacturing effort until June 1970, with the
incorporation of Prolific Designs, a much more modest project.

The second priority item in the original proposal was the Contractors'
Revolving Fund. It was argued that the black contractor was unable to bid
competitively because of lack of funds for bonding, necessary tools and
materials, and working capital to complete a project. Furthermore, since
USEDC planned to actively pursue the rehabilitation of community houses,

support of existing and new small contractors would assure that rehabilitation contracts would go to community workers. The proposed Contractors' Revolving Fund, which became a reality on May 21, 1970, was to be established to enable the contractors to borrow money from a St. Louis bank for initial bonding costs and working capital. The money was to be repaid, with interest, at the conclusion of the construction contract. The loan was secured with the contract as collateral, but was guaranteed by the Certificates of Deposit that constituted the capital investment for the revolving fund. The revolving fund was expected to increase employment, strengthen community entrepreneurs, and upgrade community skills. In addition, it had the nonmeasurable advantage of creating pride of workmanship and pride in community improvement.

In deteriorating communities, all services begin to decline as the community becomes increasingly unable to support them. Many retail establishments either fail or move into more prosperous areas, and those that remain are often unsatisfactory. During the 1960s, Union Sarah experienced a pronounced reduction in retail services, forcing residents to shop in other, more prosperous areas or to contend with inferior service and goods locally. For this reason, a shopping center was the third priority in the original proposal.

The shopping center involved almost all of the community development activities and benefits that advocates of the CDC concept had discussed. It would provide opportunities for the contractors and for all those working for contractors in construction. Shops and offices would be available for community entrepreneurs, who would benefit by the presence of strong key tenants. Community control would prevail through ownership and development of the shopping center, and profits would be used for other socially beneficial projects. In addition, goods and services would now be available to residents, and it would no longer be necessary to drive the long miles to the suburbs to shop. The shopping center has not yet become a reality, but it has been a major item on all subsequent proposals and is still considered an important priority by most residents.

The projects mentioned above were only those which USEDC participants considered most important. In addition, eight other projects were considered for inclusion in the original proposal, and nearly thirty feasibility studies were completed by the end of the second year of operation. Each proposal and feasibility study—indeed, almost every idea—was greeted with considerable enthusiasm by the staff and board members involved.

The remaining portion of this chapter discusses projects that were accepted and initiated.

Insofar as Union Sarah was not proclaimed a special impact area, and USEDC a special impact program, until June 1969, there were no measurable or visible achievements that year. The remaining months of 1969 were spent organizing a staff, establishing working committees and a community identity, and seeking new business opportunities. Still, it was a productive time, as well as one of great enthusiasm and expansiveness— and perhaps the period of greatest community involvement.

Only one major project from the original proposal was established: the Contractors' Revolving Fund. All of the other projects were finally rejected as not feasible. The board and staff soon realized that creating new businesses and acquiring viable established businesses were indeed complex and risky undertakings. Nevertheless, they continued to review proposals in an effort to invest OEO funds as efficiently and effectively as possible.

The enthusiasm and hard work of 1969 paid off in the development activities of 1970. In many ways, 1970 was the year of the greatest activity, for the largest number of ventures were started then.

At the March 1970 USEDC board of directors' meeting, three major proposals were presented: Mid-City Rentals, Prolific Designs, Inc., and the Belle Neighbors Housing Project. All three projects were approved by the board, and subsequently, Mid-City and Prolific were approved by OEO. Belle Neighbors did not require OEO approval because USEDC was to act as the developer and no investment was required.

Mid-City Rentals was acquired from Renit, Inc., an equipment rental company that had decided to divest itself of this outlet. The manager and assistant manager of the Renit operation (both blacks and now president and vice-president) invested $5,000 toward the purchase; USEDC invested $23,440; and $59,000 was borrowed from First National Bank of St. Louis. In addition, another USEDC corporation, Union Sarah Realty Investment Corporation (USRIC), was formed in June 1970, the month Mid-City opened, and bought title to the land and buildings occupied by Mid-City for $15,386.

Mid-City is an example of one of the major CDC strategies: the development of the community entrepreneur. The entrepreneur concept is based on the premise that people will work harder, and therefore better, if they have money invested in the enterprise. The chances of business success are greater under entrepreneural management than under a salaried manager. This strategy also transfers a portion of the ownership of community assets directly to a resident.

The Union Sarah Realty Investment Corporation represents still another CDC strategy, that is, that the CDC's or its subsidiary's ownership of community property provides the income necessary to invest in socially beneficial projects. Moreover, if a holding company subsidiary owns the building and property used by a business venture, the physical assets portion of the investment will remain intact should the business fail. It is also possible that the holding company will not press for rent during an unprofitable period, since the holding company and the business are owned by a common owner, the CDC. Of course, the major advantage is that the CDC will keep the property in the event the business goes bankrupt.

Prolific Designs, Inc., was also incorporated in June 1970. This enterprise, a spinoff of Monsanto Company, was originally set up to manufacture and market African art objects called Etheo Products. It had been in existence at Monsanto for about eighteen months as part of their New Enterprise Division, prior to acquisition by USEDC for $26,000. At Monsanto, the effort was labeled the ICBM (Inner City Business Mission) and had been developed through a member of Monsanto's black management personnel. When Monsanto negotiated with USEDC on the terms of transfer, it was agreed that another black Monsanto employee would become president of Prolific Designs. This project reflected the CDC's rationale on facilitating the private sector's participation with the CDC. The new president was to get stock options that would eventually permit him to buy out the USEDC financial interest.

The Belle Neighbors Housing Project, called Belle Lane Terrace, was conceived by Belle Neighbors Association working with USCC. It was a seventy-two-unit project for low-income families. Seed money was obtained through a $20,000 grant and $90,000 no-interest loan from Ralston Purina.

In November 1970, Union Sarah Leasing Corporation (USLC) was formed. Its purpose was to lease heavy equipment to Mid-City Rentals, thus expanding Mid-City's capacity without increasing its capitalization. The equipment was purchased for $28,225 from a California leasing company. USLC later leased equipment to another USEDC subsidiary, Quantum Plastics Specialties, Inc., a producer of vinyl plastisol for flexible coatings over metal, glass, paper, or fabric.

The momentum of the first two years, 1969 and 1970, continued in the early months of 1971. In January, USEDC invested $70,000 in Quantum Plastics. Quantum was an existing company, with 48 percent interest ($44,000) held by three company principals and two outside investors. Although none of the three principals was a Union Sarah resident, two were nonwhite. USEDC became involved primarily because the company would eventually be able to employ significant numbers of residents and because as a growth industry, plastics, it would produce a large return on investment. It also was an entrepreneural enterprise, allowing a small investment by the principals.

A major CDC contention is that existing black businesses often fail because they cannot obtain the financial assistance from lending institutions that is readily available to similar white businesses. In May 1971, OEO approved USEDC's establishing of a revolving loan fund for one black entrepreneural effort called Precision Tool Company, which had a cash flow problem. A $35,000 revolving loan was established to assist them during slow periods.

USEDC's most significant effort was purchased in April 1971. The building that was to house the Union Sarah/Yeatman Health Center was bought and rehabilitated for a total of $222,674. The center employs over one hundred people, many from the Union Sarah area, and provides complete health care for the residents. USEDC's offices are now located on the second floor, and a newly renovated portion of the first floor is the home of a senior citizens center.

In mid-1971, the corporation was involved with as many operating ventures and real estate efforts as it could handle. Hence, no new businesses were started in 1971 or 1972 after the investment in Quantum in early 1971. Except for Mid-City, all of the business ventures were having problems at this time; as a result, USEDC began to concentrate more on physical development and real estate.

In April 1971, the Board of Aldermen of St. Louis declared an area within Union Sarah blighted and designated it C-3 of the Neighborhood Incentive Program. USEDC, through its subsidiary USRIC, developed a proposal to build a middle-income apartment complex as the redevelopment project. OEO accepted the proposal and granted USEDC $11,000 to purchase 80 percent of the property.

Along with the project maintenance efforts of 1972, work began on a scattered-sites program. USEDC assisted in getting three houses completed during 1972 but had no equity investment in any of them. To date, no houses have been built under a scattered-site program.

In the early months of 1973, the corporation began to move in a new direction: real estate development. While this area had always been part of the overall development plan, it now became foremost in USEDC strategy. In addition to the long-awaited Belle Lane Terrace project and the C-3 Redevelopment Project, USEDC was proposing the purchase and renovation of a four-story office building called the Lister Building, the renovation of the second floor of the health center building for office space for USEDC, the complete rehabilitation of a fifty-four unit three-story apartment building (Sherwood Courts), and the initial study of a forty-acre redevelopment project. The only one of these efforts to be realized was the renovation of the second floor of the health center building. The Belle Lane Terrace Project failed to get HUD approval and had to be abandoned. The C-3 Redevelopment Project was abandoned because USEDC could not obtain mortgage insurance. Closing on the Lister Building depended on adequate leasing, and USEDC was unable to find tenants. No work was ever attempted on the forty-acre redevelopment project and, finally, Sherwood Courts had been held up because of faulty financial packaging, but it is now under construction and is expected to be completed early in 1977.

Although there was a great deal of activity in real estate development, 1973 also saw the startup of two new business ventures. In July 1973, OEO approved $110,000 for the acquisition of a carburetor rebuilding company, Union Sarah Ventures, Inc. (dba, Masco Products), and at the same time released $10,000 for the establishment of an employment service, Union Sarah Temporary Employment Service (USTES).

Masco Products employed about ten people. Acquisition of this company offered USEDC the opportunity to get involved in the auto after-market and in the apparently expanding market for rebuilt auto products. The former management was committed to stay with the operation only until new personnel were trained, but at the time of purchase there were no plans to replace any of the old employees. The only additional people hired, a manager and a bookkeeper, were hired to replace the former owner and his wife.

USTES was established as a pilot project, with only one salaried employee. The original manager was a University Year of Action (UYA) student who had also been responsible for the feasibility study. Although it was mainly an employment service for temporaries, charging clients a set daily fee, it also offered clients the option of employing any temporary worker on a full-time basis, at no fee. During the temporary period, the client was to pay a fee to USTES, who then would pay the wages of the temporary help. If the client found the temporary worker to be a good employee, he could offer permenent employment and cease paying a fee to USTES at that point. After the first year of operation, thirty people had found full-time employment, and between fifteen and twenty people per day got temporary work. The staff had been increased to two salaried employees and one UYA student.

In 1974, USEDC continued in its real estate objectives but without success. Efforts to find viable business ventures were also continued. Most of USEDC's energies were expended monitoring existing ventures.

In June 1974, USEDC opened a supermarket with an investment of $156,500. The store, named Union Sarah Community Foods and doing business as Union Sarah Community IGA, was located in the building that formerly housed a Kroger store. It was hoped that this community-controlled store would eliminate the problems of overcharging and poor-quality merchandising in area stores. It would also eliminate the necessity of shopping for food in the suburbs. Finally, a community store would have more knowledge of the eating habits of the population and would thus get proper stocks.

In the remaining months of 1974, the business ventures, particularly the new supermarket, were monitored and future development plans were formulated.

On January 6, 1975, OEO advised USEDC that their refunding proposal was to be submitted by January 30, rather than March 30 as previously projected. Allowing for some board participation and internal approvals, the staff had only twenty-four days to prepare a proposal for a two-year period. The proposal, as submitted, was rejected by OEO, and USEDC was placed on a no-cost extension, that is, they were granted no new funds but were permitted to continue operations with carryover funds from the past two-year period. The no-cost extension was for the seven-month period June through December, at which time a second proposal would be considered, providing USEDC met the stipulated conditions established by OEO. The major conditions were an update of resumes and job descriptions, a staff and board training proposal, the submittal of an overall economic development plan (OEDP), and the improvement of staff and board relationships as well as an indication of overall improved efficiency.

A large amount of staff time was devoted to answering OEO communications in 1975 and attempting to meet the conditions of the no-cost extension. Although some work toward new ventures was accomplished, no new business development was started in 1975. The real estate staff received board and OEO approval for the rehabilitation of sixteen dwelling units on what was termed a force account project, meaning that the units would be built with 100 percent USEDC-invested money and no attempt would be made to leverage through lending institutions.

By the end of 1975, two subsidiary corporations, Union Sarah Foods, Inc., and Quantum Plastics Specialties, Inc., failed and were closed. Masco Products was in serious trouble, and Mid-City Rentals experienced large losses in their second store and was having overall difficulties.

In December 1975, USEDC's proposal for the period January 1, 1976, through December 31, 1977, was approved for $1.5 million. The approval specified that USEDC must meet the agreed-upon project milestones, as set forth in the OEO portion of their proposal.

USEDC attempted in every way to follow the concept of the CDC as established by the legislation and as elucidated by the CDC advocates. Throughout the six years of operation covered in this study, those involved with USEDC maintained their enthusiasm and faith in the program. They strove to achieve maximum community control, employ as many residents as possible, encourage entrepreneurship, and gain control of community assets for profits for the community. In addition, every effort was made to involve the private sector and local government in USEDC; for the most part, however, assistance simply did not materialize.

Of the projects started during 1969-1976—Prolific Designs, Quantum Plastics, Mid-City Rentals, Union Sarah Temporary Employment Service, Masco Products, and Union Sarah Community Foods—only Mid-City is still in business. Mid-City Rentals can be classed as marginal. Certainly, this record is far removed from what Stewart Perry and Geoffrey Faux projected, not to mention Hampden-Turner's expectations.

The results of the USEDC efforts over these past years are shown in Table 5. The reasons for the program's failure will be analyzed in the detailed case study in Chapter 4. At this point, it seems fair to question whether USEDC's failure to bring about the community benefits expected by Hampden-Turner and others was the result of the St. Louis participants' ineptitude or the result of inherent failings and contradictions of the CDC concept itself. This question will be explored in the following chapter.

NOTES

1. Taken from SIP 1, the Union Sarah proposal to OEO for initial funding, pp. iv, 1, 2.
2. Ibid., p. iv-3.

Table 5

USEDC INVESTMENT AND RETURNS

June 1969 to December 1975

Project	Investment	Profit	Loss	Total Employees	Total Resident Employees
Prolific Designs	$163,000	0	$163,000	Bankrupt	—
Quantum Plastics	170,000	0	170,000	Failed	—
Mid-City Rentals	119,940	15,000	0	10	4
USTES*	10,000	0	10,000	Failed	—
Masco	110,000	0	78,000	3	0
Supermarket	206,500	0	206,500	Failed	—
USLC	28,225	0	0	0	0
USRIC					
Commercial**	238,060	110,960	0	104	—
Sherwood	200,000	0	0	0	—
C-3 Project	48,000	0	0	0	—
Scattered Site	37,500	0	0	0	—
Force Account	210,371	0	0	4	2
Loan Funds					
Contractors' Revolving***	100,000	0	59,000	0	—
Precision Tool	35,000	0	18,200	Discontinued	—
USEDC	NA	NA	NA	12	1
Totals	$1,676,596	$125,960	$704,721	133	7

* USTES generated twenty-five full-time positions with outside clients for Union Sarah residents.
** Employment reflected is health center employment.
*** The loan fund assisted in creating contracts and temporary employment not reflected in this table.

4

CDC CONCEPTS AND STRATEGIES APPLIED TO USEDC

This chapter examines the concepts and strategies of community economic development as they were applied to USEDC and evaluates their effectiveness. Although each is examined separately, all touch on elements of the others; therefore, the general discussions will overlap.

COMMUNITY CONTROL

Those who advocate the CDC point to community control as the major factor separating it from other poverty programs. The community control argument has the following implications:

1. That the general community population, especially the poor, are involved in directing the activities of the corporation.

2. That community people have the leading policy and decision-making roles in the CDC. That community people also play key roles in subsidiary efforts created by the CDC.

3. That, as an extension of the above, these community people will gradually rise to be the policy and decision-makers for the community, and outsiders will only assist and advise.

4. That, through community control of community business and physical assets, profits now accruing to people from outside the area will be retained for reinvestment and for socially beneficial activities. This reinvestment will further extend community control.

Those who established USEDC accepted the above implications and attempted to organize USEDC in accordance with community control. Already in existence when USEDC arrived was the Neighborhood Advisory Council (NAC), which is an informal group whose main requirements for membership are residency within the community and age (sixteen years or older). NAC holds annual elections and also nominates members of the community to stand for USCC board election. Another group that was already in existence was the Union Sarah Community Corporation, whose board members are nominated by NAC and elected by a community-wide election. Every resident and person employed in the Union Sarah area sixteen years of age or older is eligible to vote and hold office.

Sixty thousand shares of stock were authorized at $1 par value per share for the incorporation of USEDC. OEO granted USCC 30,001 shares to insure that control of the corporation would always remain with the community. As the majority stockholder, USCC controls the board membership of USEDC. The USEDC board consists of twenty-nine members; fifteen are elected by the USCC board, and the remaining fourteen by a nominating committee from the USEDC sitting board and elected at the annual stockholders' meeting. It was anticipated that these members would be drawn from the greater St. Louis business, academic, political, and social leadership.

In addition, it was planned to sell stock to the community residents at $1 per share. Although the sale of stock cannot be limited to the community by law, advertising and efforts to sell would be limited to the community. Ownership of stock would instill interest and encourage further resident participation in USEDC as well as strengthen the community control aspect. This stock was made available to insure that the general community population would become involved in directing USEDC activities.

USEDC planned to appoint community people to the corporation staff at all levels, to the extent possible. There were also many discussions concerning training, upward mobility of staff members, and both vertical and horizontal transfers between the CDC and CDC subsidiaries and between one subsidiary and another. It was thought that this arrangement would provide optimum opportunity for residents to take responsible decision-making roles.

As subsidiary efforts could take several directions, in each case plans were made for resident participation at all levels. The entrepreneural concept assumed that a resident would be the entrepreneur and would be given both financial and technical assistance by the CDC. In his capacity as entrepreneur, he would direct the activities of his business, become independent of white or outside domination, and participate in business activities within the greater community. In the joint ventures, all management positions would be filled by men from the community and from the corporation involved. This situation would continue until the community people could take over without assistance. Finally, in acquisitions, the policy established was that a management component from the original company would remain long enough to train new management. In the case of completely new startups, the corporate policy was to find competent people from the community for all positions, or at least blacks. If no qualified person in either category could be found, then the corporation could hire a qualified person from any source.

By assuming board or staff roles, the community would build a broad-based leadership group, which would work for the best interests of the community. Training programs were planned for all management levels in order to give the employees experience and familiarity with theory. The training programs were to include St. Louis business and academic resources and would encompass board and staff responsibilities, financial analysis, communication skills, and personnel management. Plans were also made to bring in national CDC figures to relate the experience of other CDCs and familiarize USEDC people with accepted interpretations of the CDC movement.

At the very beginning it was envisioned that USEDC would eventually control a large portion of the community assets and be a major employer in the area. To accomplish real control and gain the best utilization of profits, USEDC corporations would supply and purchase from one another. Thus, supportive corporations such as Union Sarah Leasing Corporation (USLC), Union Sarah Realty Investment Corporation (USRIC), and the Contractors' Revolving Loan Fund came into being. When a new business was started, USRIC could lessen the debt service of the new business by purchasing the property to house it, while USLC could lessen the debt service or investment level by purchasing the necessary equipment and leasing it to the new company. Hence, the business would have a little better chance of surviving, and at the same time both USRIC and USLC were receiving support and growth opportunities. Another benefit would be that rental and leasing fees would remain in the community. The Contractors' Revolving Fund was to provide loans to give black contractors an opportunity to bid on projects previously out of their reach; the payback and interest would remain in the community.

As profits from the various enterprises grew, USEDC could provide the finances to support the community's social welfare efforts. In addition, developing institutions would give the community a power base for asking the city for a bigger share of St. Louis's welfare programs.

As regards benefits derived from utilizing facilities efficiently, an example is USEDC's renovation of the second floor of the health center for its corporate offices. The conference room is used not only by USEDC, but also by various community groups.

All of the above shows that USEDC has been faithful to the concepts of community control, and that there have always been plans and attempts to involve community residents. Now we will examine what has actually occurred over the years to determine to what extent community control really exists, and, if it does exist, how it translates as control by the poor.

As previously mentioned, at first USEDC had broad community support from existing organizations. This support, however, did not necessarily represent the poor. Union Sarah, like most communities, is not a one-class, single-purpose community; rather, it is made up of people representing various interests and groups. It has a significant middle class made up of property owners and professional and business leaders. It also has a large number of poor people. The middle-class element most participates in the USEDC's activities. For example, the board of directors shows a membership of bankers, teachers, ministers, politicians, and community business people. (See Tables 6 and 7.)

Table 6

1971 USEDC BOARD MEMBERSHIP

Occupation	Number of People	Residents
Businessman	5	5
Quality control	1	1
Maintenance man	1	1
State representative	3	2
Minister	2	1
Newspaper editor	1	1
Teamster	1	1
Educator	4	2
Insurance agent	1	1
Banker	1	0
Manager	1	0
Alderman	1	1
Welfare worker	1	1
Pharmacist	1	0
City employee	1	0
Student	1	1
Total	26*	18

*Three board vacancies.

Table 7

1974 USEDC BOARD MEMBERSHIP

Occupation	Number of People	Residents
Businessman	8	7
Quality control	1	1
Maintenance man	1	1
State representative	2	2
Teamster	1	1
Educator	4	3
Alderman	1	1
Student	1	1
Homemaker	3	3
Manager	1	1
Banker	1	0
Welfare worker	1	1
Retired	2	2
Total	27	24

An analysis of Tables 6 and 7 shows that community participation on
USEDC's board of directors increased from 68 percent in 1971 to 88 percent in 1974. The goal of attracting professional and business leaders
from the greater St. Louis community has not been achieved, however.
None of the board members can be described as poor: they are community
leaders, educators, legislators, and business people.

Many of the board members attend meetings only rarely and when
they do attend are not active participants. It is difficult to arrive at a
quorum for most board meetings, and committee meetings are even harder
to arrange. Indeed, no more than half a dozen members can be said to
have significant influence on the board.

An index of community participation can be surmised from the following statement about USEDC from a report on CDCs by Abt Associations:
"fewer than 2% of total respondents in January, 1973, were able to identify
the CDC—a result of USEDC's low profile approach."[1] Another indication
comes from an October 1974 study conducted by students of the Sociology
Department at Washington University. With the assistance of the USEDC
staff the students developed a questionnaire for use in the Union Sarah
area. Of fifty-one respondents to the question "Have you heard of the
Union Sarah Economic Development Corporation?," thirty-four answered
yes and seventeen no. Of those respondents, not one could give the name
of the director of USEDC. Twenty-four respondents had heard of the
Union Sarah IGA; twenty had heard of the temporary employment service;
but only five had heard of the health center. No other USEDC projects
were identified. This study was conducted only four blocks from the
USEDC and the health center.

The total community has only an indirect input into USEDC board
membership through their part in electing USCC board members, from
which a majority of USEDC board members are chosen. The extent of
community participation, even indirectly, is reflected in Table 8, which
shows the number of residents employed in the area, over sixteen years
of age, who have voted in each of the past elections. Since the estimated
population of eligible voters is 20,000, only about 15 percent typically
cast votes.

Whether community control can exist with such low-level participation
is, of course, questionable. The participation that does exist is not that of
poor people, but of a few business-oriented residents.

The level of resident employment on the USEDC staff and with the

Table 8

NUMBERS VOTING IN USCC ELECTIONS

Year	Total Votes
1968	Not available
1969	2,324
1970	Not available
1971	Not available
1972	4,097
1973	Not available
1974	2,776

subsidiary operations is another indication of community control. Table 9 shows, by corporation, the number of employees, residents, and management positions held by residents. The term *manager* is used to denote executive positions.

As shown in the table, of the total enrollment at USEDC and USEDC subsidiaries, only five of twenty-two people, or 23 percent are Union Sarah residents. Of six in management positions, two are residents. Table 9 indicates that USEDC has not been successful in getting residents staff positions. At USEDC, as in any corporation, those who make the day-to-day decisions have significant control over the corporation, even though that control is not ultimate control. Because they have greater familiarity with the problems, more data, and a posture of knowledgeability, senior staff members wield significant influence over board decisions, as well as direct decision-making power over day-to-day happenings. USEDC is thus

Table 9

USEDC STAFF AND SUBSIDIARY EMPLOYMENT

Corporation	Number of Employees	Number of Residents	Number of Managers	Resident Managers
USEDC	12	1	4	1
Mid-City Rentals	10	4	2	1
Total	22	5	6	2

failing to train policy and decision-makers for the community. They have also failed to place residents in key roles in the subsidiary operations: only one subsidiary, Mid-City, has a resident in a key management position.

There are only two residents who are managers with either USEDC or its subsidiaries. One of the two, the president at USEDC, is the single most powerful person in the total structure. But, of course, this does not represent broad-based control by a large portion of the residents. Unfortunately, it is nearly impossible to find managers from the resident population. Those who could have qualified have either fled the community or now hold positions with salaries beyond what USEDC or its subsidiaries could pay.

An example of the problem can be illustrated by Masco's experience. At the time it was acquired, USEDC was assured by the seller that an adequate management component would remain to train replacement management. USEDC interviewed residents and found a highly recommended person who lacked experience but had the necessary enthusiasm, interest, and intelligence to learn. The management component that remained, however, was not trustworthy and did not get along with the other employees. The new manager's lack of management experience made it impossible for him to cope with the problems of production, sales, and purchasing. As a result, Masco suffered a $42,000 loss in the first year. This subsidiary has since failed.

With regard to CDC's theory that community control will be extended by the reinvestment of profits into new businesses, the facts are very bleak. From June 1969 to December 1975, with an investment of $1,678,000 USEDC had a net loss of about $705,000 (Table 5). Further analysis will indicate that the one remaining venture, Mid-City, will not produce profits for reinvestment in the community.

The facts can be summarized as follows:

1. Only a very small portion of the residents actually has influence over the corporation.

2. USEDC has failed to employ residents in decision-making positions and has hired relatively few residents in *any* capacity. Therefore, the residents' managerial influence is small.

3. Few poor residents are involved with the corporation in any way.

4. Ventures have not been profitable and therefore have not increased the strength of the community.

The single most important aspect of community control has never been mentioned by the CDC advocates. Simply put, it is that *inner-city communities do not contain the resources necessary for community development.* The Union Sarah area, as is true of most inner-city poverty areas, is in a negative resource position. The liabilities of the community are greater than the assets to the degree that development within free enterprise capitalism is not possible.

Finally, any assessment of CDC must go back to the objectives of SIP 1. The first objective was to develop large or medium-sized manufacturing firms. The state of manufacturing in the 1970s demands efficient, one-story, "in one end and out the other" facilities that take up a great deal of space. This type of facility is necessary if one is to compete. But the buildings in the Union Sarah area are multi-story, inefficient, light-manufacturing facilities that date from the turn of the century or the 1920s or 1930s. Anyone would hesitate to establish a labor-intensive manufacturing plant there.

The second objective, the Contractor's Revolving Loan Fund, was established in May 1970. The primary purpose was to provide operating capital for small contractors living or employed in the Union Sarah district. Through certificates of deposit, USEDC guaranteed the bank loans made to contractors, thereby enabling these contractors, who were high-risk borrowers, to bid on contracts previously beyond their potential because lending institutions refused to lend them money. The fund had to be discontinued because of loan defaults of over $60,000. The defaults were a result of the contractors' inexperience in bidding for jobs, planning, meeting commitments, keeping records, and general business acumen. Even so, a fair number of construction jobs resulted from this effort, and it is hoped that some small contractors have been given an opportunity to exist and perhaps succeed as a result.

The third objective was the development of a shopping center. A successful shopping center must have a large, economically viable market. Also, the center's owners must be able to acquire the property and build the center at a cost that is low enough for them to lease it competitively. Finally, there must be a key tenant that will attract other tenants and the necessary market. Union Sarah, like most other inner-city areas, lacks all of these ingredients necessary for success.

The fourth objective, to provide seed money to expand existing resident-owned businesses and to establish new businesses, was never attempted, because all development efforts failed to produce profits that could be used for this purpose. Staff efforts were totally committed to making a success of USEDC corporate-owned enterprises and to seeking new opportunities for corporate investments. Efforts to seek out and assist resident-owned businesses never gained sufficient support, and there were few, if any, requests for assistance from community business owners. If this objective had been pursued, it is not likely that it would have succeeded, due to the business climate of the area.

The development and training of community people to staff USEDC and its subsidiaries, the fifth objective, has been a continuing effort. Very few community people have been employed, however, as there have been few opportunities for them, and therefore training has not improved community skills to any extent. One important exception is provided by the president of USEDC, who is a resident. He has had significant training from both formal training programs and the experience of being the chief executive. Indeed, he has showed both personal and professional growth.

The sixth objective, to participate in and have some control over business operations within the total area, has not been achieved. USEDC efforts failed, but even had they been successful, the scope of that objective is too broad to be accomplished, except in a minor sense. Each business developed is a partial achievement of this objective, but real control requires ownership of hundreds of businesses, large and small, and is simply beyond resources of a CDC.

The seventh objective, to foster a policy that will attract major companies to the area, has always existed. However, the CDC was never successful in attracting business, since the area is not perceived as a viable business area.

The eighth objective was to coordinate the efforts of other community organizations in the economic area. Attempts were made to obtain such coordination through a businessman's association. However, community businessmen were not willing to participate in a meaningful way, by committing the necessary time and money to such an association, and therefore these efforts failed.

The ninth and tenth objectives merely call for the demonstrated success of the CDC. At this time, neither has been achieved, and they are not likely to be achieved in the future.

When factors such as higher insurance rates, high crime, poor police protection, inadequate fire protection, deteriorating environment, and decreasing middle class are added in, then the picture of community resources becomes clear. The most decisive factor of community control, resources that permit development, is simply not available in the Union Sarah community.

The final factor relating to control concerns the agent with final responsibility for releasing funds. For USEDC this final authority rests with OEO. The community, or whatever element participates, has control only after the funds are released and the venture is established—and then often with limiting conditions set by OEO.

THE ENTREPRENEURAL STRATEGY

Of major importance to the concept of community control is the entrepreneural strategy. This strategy is at the heart of efforts to develop black capitalism and was important to the early OEO ideas of community control. In cases where community members own the community businesses, employ other residents, buy from other community entrepreneurs, and reinvest profits in the community, control of the community rests with the community members. In contrast are cases wherein the absentee white owners take out of the community whatever profit is derived from its assets.

The CDC assumes that the entrepreneur would be more likely to make a business successful than the hired manager because the entrepreneur would have a vested interest. CDC's role in this strategy is to enable community members to become entrepreneurs by assisting in capitalization of enterprises, providing technical assistance, and adding the weight of its support for market development and preferential treatment.

Through enterpreneurship, the community entrepreneur would gain experience in business, become more independent, and improve both his self-image and his standing in the community. In addition, CDC advocates state that when the entrepreneur is on equal terms with white businessmen,[2] racial integration is promoted.

As stated earlier, OEO very much favored entrepreneurship in the early years of the CDC; the first USEDC director also believed strongly in its validity. Therefore, despite the implications of labor intensivity found in the original proposal, USEDC was well disposed toward the entrepreneural strategy.

What can be said for the successful business ventures started by USEDC? Mid-City Rentals is USEDC's only successful business. In the summer of 1974, Mid-City opened a second store, and it now employs a total of ten people. Since its inception, it has produced a profit of $15,000. (Since the second store has been in operation, it has suffered small monthly losses.)

Mid-City is an example of the correct approach to an entrepreneural effort. Mid-City was successful under its previous owners and had always shown a modest profit. It had a good business reputation and an established clientele. It is located on a major artery and in a part of the Union Sarah community that has a large, stable working population. More important, the entrepreneurs are experienced managers who have had years of experience in the business at that location and with the same clients. Mid-City remains USEDC's best managed and only profitable business.[3]

In contrast, a second venture, Prolific Designs, Inc., had all the ingredients for failure. It was not strictly entrepreneural in that the company president had no investment position. Even so, PDI embraced the entrepreneural philosophy. A stock purchase program was initiated to provide the president with ownership, and the long-range plan called for his eventual control and possible takeover of the company. Unfortunately, the ingredients that were present in Mid-City did not exist in this new effort. PDI had been in existence as part of the New Enterprise Division of Monsanto for about eighteen months prior to acquisition and was presented to USEDC as one of several efforts by Monsanto to "do something" about the urban crisis. The firm had all the earmarks of success; i.e., a presumably positive market research, product development, established distribution system, and assurances of Monsanto's confidence in the project.

When promotion and sales did not result in the expected volume, PDI found it necessary to drop the African art object line and expand into the plastic coating market. A total of $25,000 was approved on November 6, 1970, for this expansion, but was increased to $40,000 and approved by OEO in December. The expansion was expected to increase employment from twelve to twenty-five people.

Throughout the period June 1971 to April 1973, a special task force consisting of a senior staff member and executives from Monsanto and McDonnell-Douglas worked unsuccessfully to bring stability to PDI. In May 1973, the corporation filed for bankruptcy. The PDI board of directors held a special meeting on June 15, 1973, for the purposes of terminating operation and protecting the remaining assets for the benefit of the creditors.

PDI was almost programmed for failure. It had inexperienced management, and the company was unknown. In addition, the market research provided by Monsanto was, at the very least, faulty. The major point here is not to cite management flaws but to emphasize that entrepreneural efforts must be confined to businesses that are within the scope of the entrepreneur's skills and experience. Otherwise, entrepreneurship has no chance of succeeding. Also, new, unfamiliar businesses should be viewed as high risks.

Quantum is perhaps the best example of the weakness of the entrepreneural approach to community development. The business did not employ even one community resident, and it existed primarily for the benefit of two minority entrepreneurs.

In March 1971, just prior to the SIP 11 funding period, Quantum attempted to expand into plastic fabrications, as being complementary to the plastisol formulation business. They secured several large contracts to produce plastic traffic cones, but their technology and product quality did not measure up to market demands and the contracts were canceled. The resulting loss put the company into a vulnerable position, and a minority stockholder moved to take over the company in a forced stock sale at a much reduced price. He held a $15,000 note and threatened to call it in, forcing the company into bankruptcy if his terms were not met. An emergency loan was obtained from Ralston Purina to satisfy the outstanding note and provide immediate cash flow, while the staff arranged, through a proposal to OEO, for the release of $100,000 of venture funds to stabilize Quantum.

As a condition of the $100,000 grant, Quantum was directed to return to the formulation of plastisols only, which was done. This did not end the corporation's problems, however, and it continued to suffer losses through June 1972. The plastisol business increased, and large orders began coming in from one customer. This customer was on a ninety-day pay agreement, and this large account began to seriously affect Quantum's cash flow. Although enjoying a brief seller's market during most of 1974, in 1975 Quantum had a cash flow problem. Late in 1975, it closed for a loss of $170,000.

In May 1971, OEO approved a $35,000 grant to establish a revolving loan fund for one company's use, the Precision Tool Company. This was an entrepreneural effort that had sought assistance from USEDC and had proposed a USEDC investment for expanded capability and business stability. This project was considered to be viable and to offer residents the opportunity to become involved in tool and die making and the machinist trade generally. OEO advised USEDC not to invest but approved assistance with a revolving loan. The company, located near the Union Sarah area and black-owned, was a machine tool and die and metal fabricator which was doing business with the Coast Guard and Kaiser Refractories, Inc. The company was unable to meet orders and lost both the Coast Guard and Kaiser accounts. The company subsequently failed, and the revolving loan fund terminated with a $15,000 loss.

In all of the studies of entrepreneural efforts by USEDC, USEDC has had the major shareholder position. In this sense, none of the projects was truly entrepreneural. As the major shareholder, USEDC has also monitored each of the ventures, and members of its board of directors hold a majority position on all of the boards.

In its purest form, the entrepreneural effort would demand that control be in the hands of the entrepreneur. The CDC would be an enabler, either through providing seed money in the form of a loan or a grant or acting as a guarantor to a lending institution, as was the case with the Contractors' Revolving Loan Fund.

Nevertheless, the projects mentioned here followed the philosophy of entrepreneurship, and the managers involved considered themselves entrepreneurs. Regardless of philosophy, the problems inherent in small business in today's competitive markets have proved massive and, as noted above, only Mid-City has been even marginally successful.

The reasons why USEDC's projects failed are many and complex, but the single most important reason is lack of management experience and skills. The small entrepreneur, even more than the large corporation, must be familiar with every aspect of his business. He needs to know his market and his clients, and he must have a reputation for dependability. He must know his accounting principles, the state of the art in whatever technology involved, and how to set up his operation efficiently. All of these skills take years of experience to develop; technical know-how from the outside will not make up for lack of this experience. Most of all, the small entrepreneur must have the commitment necessary to put in the time and work needed to succeed.

In today's economy, the small businessman is at a distinct disadvantage. He pays more for raw materials because he buys at a lower volume. He has trouble getting credit and often must pay COD for deliveries; on the other hand, he often has to wait for his orders. As a result, he has a continual cash flow problem. The lending institutions are of little help, for they look at the small, tenuous business as a high risk. The CDC small business, located in the inner city, has the additional disadvantages of obsolete facilities, high insurance rates, high crime, poor transportation, unskilled and poorly motivated employees, and, if dealing in a retail business, an undercapitalized market.

SUPPORT FROM THE PRIVATE SECTOR

At the time of USEDC's inception in mid-1969, every segment of the greater St. Louis community, from Civic Progress[4] to Junior Achievement, pledged its support. For example, the Municipal Business Development Commission pledged technical assistance equaling $6,000. The Small Business Administration promised loan assistance counseling programs. The Regional Industrial Development Corporation's executive director agreed to serve on the new corporation's Technical Assistance Committee and to write a strong letter of support. The Business Advisory Teams pledged active support, as did Black Enterprise Today, the Urban League, CORE, YMCA, and the Neighborhood Youth Corps, as well as Monsanto, McDonnell-Douglas, and other large corporations. All major St. Louis universities offered assistance as did ten area churches. In short, the leadership of St. Louis as well as that of the Union Sarah community strongly supported the idea of community economic development. It was a period when business leaders across the country were proclaiming their company's social responsibility in speeches, articles, and annual reports. It was popular for businesses to promise support of black capitalism and of the minority communities' programs.

On the government level, Congress continued to press for private sector support of minority communities, as indicated in the following paragraph from the Community Self-Determination Act of 1969:

> The private enterprise system and the independent sector
> should be offered new incentives to join with the people
> of a community in a partnership for individual and com-
> munity improvement, especially in providing technical and
> managerial expertise, offering training for jobs with a future,
> providing investment capital, and building productive plants
> and facilities for sale to members of the community. Such a

> program should be designed to permit the people of a com-
> munity-sponsored enterprises to provide needed social serv-
> ice, thereby reducing the burden of taxation upon the rest
> of society.[5]

As a result, CDCs across the country were optimistic, and justifiably so, about assistance from private corporations. The Xerox Corporation and FIGHT, a black community organization, announced plans for an electrical transformer and metal stamping plant in Rochester, New York, in June 1968.[6] This and similar planned projects were given considerable news coverage in those early days of the CDCs. The leadership of Union Sarah was no different from that of the other CDCs. It actively courted local businessmen, seeking technical assistance, advisors for board participation, joint venture opportunities, preferential market treatment, and an opportunity to convince them to build plants or locate in existing facilities within the Union Sarah area.

During the first years of operation, the president of USEDC expended a considerable public relations effort on gaining support from the leadership of St. Louis, particularly the business leadership. He became a member of the St. Louis Chamber of Commerce in the hope of eliciting support from business leaders with whom he might come in contact. There was some private sector interest in those formative months in the form of technical assistance committee membership and letters of support. However, the technical assistance committee never really became operational and the early enthusiasm soon evaporated.

The earliest, and still the most prevalent, support from the private sector was participation on either the USEDC board of directors or a subsidiary board. Both Monsanto Company and McDonnell-Douglas Corporation were represented on the board of Prolific Designs, Inc., and both provided technical assistance to PDI. While it was in no way a great amount of help, it did involve several hours each week for one, or at times two, men from each company. Much of this time was personal and therefore was at no cost to the companies. In addition, Monsanto provided PDI with some industrial spray painting subcontracts as part of the last-ditch effort to save the company from bankruptcy.

The most impressive assistance was provided by Ralston Purina in the form of a $20,000 outright grant and a $90,000 no-interest loan to the

Belle Neighbors project.[7] As previously mentioned, Ralston also gave a quick, short-term, no-interest loan of $25,000 to USEDC to provide the necessary capital to ward off a takeover of Quantum Plastics by a minority stockholder. The assistance provided by Ralston on the Belle Neighbors project gave USEDC its first active role in real estate development. Even though Belle Lane Terrace, the project's official name, was never able to get off the ground, this first step into real estate resulted in the creation of a real estate department and the eventual purchase of a building to house the Union Sarah/Yeatman Health Center.

Although USEDC has always attempted to involve the private sector in developmental activities, particularly the larger St. Louis-based corporations, a special effort was made in 1973. As the director of venture formation and management, I assisted the president in his efforts to encourage private sector participation. The strategy formulated was to provide private sector organizations, through their chief executives and other selected executives, as well as key government officeholders, with as much information on USEDC activities as possible. This was accomplished through personal contacts, after which a followup letter was sent, and through a mailing of selected information to a mailing list of thirty-five important St. Louis leaders. In response to about 175 letters sent out, USEDC received twenty-eight letters from fifteen sources. Interviews with Southwestern Bell, Ralston Purina, Monsanto, and McDonnell-Douglas Corporation can also be attributed to this effort. Four articles were prepared for an area monthly newspaper, *The West End Word.* Each of these articles went to the parties on the mailing list, along with the corporation's annual report, a copy of the USEDC newsletter, and other material from business magazines on corporate responsibility. Letters were sent out in January, February, March, April, June, August, and December 1973. Although a few responses were received, the only tangible result was the aforementioned meetings. The following letter and enclosure led to the initial meetings with the four companies mentioned above.

> Dear Mr.   :
> In a continuing effort to gain your support, and that of other
> St. Louis community leaders, I wish to share these enclosures.
> I hope that you find them informative, and possibly thought-
> provoking. The first is an article from *Saturday Review of the*

Society, the April edition, which contains a special business supplement, "Can The Businessman Meet Our Social Needs?". I recommend the entire supplement and wish that I could have afforded to send it to you complete. However, the article, "The Possibilities of Partnership" is of special interest, in that it reflects in part the present direction of USEDC.

The West End Word, a small but influential St. Louis monthly, contains an article that explicitly states our position.

I hope that sometime we might discuss potential ways to become involved in a joint effort to effect some change in the Union-Sarah area. Your consideration will be most appreciated.

Very truly yours,
/s/ H. E. Berndt, Director
Venture Formation Management

"Union-Sarah Economic Develop Corp. Works for Area Improvement"
Blight and the concomitant evils of crime and disease are on the increase in cities across the country. In St. Louis, as in most other major cities, the conditions under which many people live strains the credulity of even the most callous. And yet many in our city have more and live better than their fathers ever dreamed. But these enclaves of relative well being become fewer each year while those of poverty increase. This article concerns one effort, that of the Union-Sarah Economic Development Corporation (USEDC) to reclaim the city as a viable community for all who live within its boundaries.

For those not familiar with USEDC, it is a St. Louis-based community development corporation funded by a $2.1 million grant from the Office of Economic Opportunity. It is a for-profit corporation dedicated to improve the economic conditions of its residents through creating new businesses and encouraging others to locate in the Union-Sarah area, and by assisting, financially and otherwise,

existing business. To this end USEDC has established subsidiary corporations in real estate investment and development, manufacturing, and retail business, and has assisted
small contractors and business by providing low interest
loans and technical help. It has been unsuccessful in attracting other new business, and is less than satisfied with its impact
on area unemployment.

One of 42 community economic development corporations
across the nation, USEDC faces those problems endemic to
all efforts created to alleviate poverty; e.g., lack of technical
assistance, insufficient community support, and a large dose
of that deadly small business disease, economic Darwinism.
USEDC has learned that although small business efforts are
fine, and entrepreneurship has its value, effective economic
development demands projects that are labor intensive. In
short, employment is the name of the game. Also, the experience of community development corporations nation-wide
indicates that efforts of this magnitude are possible only
when those who control the markets, the large corporations,
are involved.

In 1971, nine major St. Louis based corporations spent a
total of $810,836,000 in capital expenditures—i.e., new plants
and additions. Of this amount, $200,000 was spent in the
city of St. Louis, none of which was labor generating. These
same corporations enjoyed sales of almost $11 billion and
profits of over $897 million. Recent news releases indicate
that in the coming year the story will be the same, as one
company has announced plans for new plant construction of
nearly $100 million and another company announced a projected
expenditure of $160 million, none of which is likely to be desig-
nated for the city of St. Louis. It seems reasonable to ask, why
is this?

Are the corporations going to abandon the city of St. Louis,
or will they recognize that they are public as well as private
and that poverty, disease and crime are their concern as well
as the concern of each of us as individuals?

USEDC is asking that St. Louis corporations join with them
in stemming the tide of unemployment and city blight by
1) Participating in joint ventures with USEDC to establish plants
in the area, 2) Provide sub-contracts so that USEDC can create
new manufacturing efforts, or, 3) Establish plants in the Union-
Sarah area instead of Florida, Georgia, or wherever.

To west end residents, we appeal for support in our efforts to
convince our major corporations that their welfare and best
interests are tied not just in profits, but to the health and vitality
of the total community.

The meetings with the corporations emphasized the need for greater corporate involvement in the inner city, and in each case there was general agreement that the private sector should probably be more involved. The corporations emphasized that their primary objective was profits and their first
responsibility to stockholders. They pointed out that they hired minorities,
used minority firms as vendors when they could find them, supported the
United Fund, Urban League, and Negro College Fund, and were large local
employers. Several meetings with McDonnell-Douglas were to no avail because at the time they had not completed an audit and evaluation of corporate involvement by their Corporate Responsibility Committee. They stated
that since changing or establishing new policy takes considerable time,
they would not be able to participate in USEDC's activity.

USEDC was attempting to interest corporations in a joint venture plan
whereby both USEDC and the subject corporation would invest capital, the
subject corporation would provide a management component until the new
community management could function independently, and a protected
market would be provided to a breakeven point, until enough other business
was captured to sustain the new corporation. Another possibility mentioned
was the location of a subsidiary plant in the Union Sarah area or the provision of subcontracts for existing CDC companies. These very suggestions had
been carried out by other corporations in other locations; in fact, McDonnell-Douglas was involved in a joint venture project in Watts.

The kind of replies received and followup action taken can be seen in the
following response by Southwestern Bell Telephone to the initial letter:

R. R. Shockley
Vice President, Missouri-Illinois

March 30, 1973

Dear Mr. Berndt:

Mr. Alston referred your letter of March 14 to me since I have
the responsibility for all activities of our company in the state
of Missouri. I read the two articles you attached to your letter
with great interest. I certainly agree with the basic message of
both—the necessity for business to become more involved in
the communities where it operates. We at Southwestern Bell
have followed this idea for many years and have continually
increased our participation. We would like to do even more,
but our present earnings do not allow us this luxury. Mr.
Robert Bannecker, 247-3522, who has the assignment of
Urban Affairs for our St. Louis Area, will be glad to assist you
in any way he can.

Sincerely,

/s/ R. R. Shockley

Upon receipt of Mr. Shockley's letter, a meeting was arranged between
myself and Mr. Bannecker. The purpose of the meeting was to determine
what, if anything, Southwestern Bell could do to assist in USEDC's programs. Most of the interview consisted of a litany of Southwestern Bell's
employee volunteer activities, which Southwestern Bell claims as a major
portion of its social responsibility programs.

The following month, USEDC took an option on an office building
and was attempting to attract an adequate number of tenants to make
the purchase feasible. To this end another article was written for *The
West End Word,* advertisements were placed in several papers, and letters
were written to mailing list parties. The following letter was sent to
Southwestern Bell:

Dear Mr. Shockley:

Some time ago I had the pleasure of visiting with Mr. Robert
Bannecker, your Urban Affairs Supervisor, as a result of a
letter I had written to Mr. Alston. I discussed with Mr. Bannecker
the plans and programs of Union-Sarah Economic Development
Corporation, as well as something of the history and development of our corporation. We also talked in a general way about

ways in which Southwestern Bell and Union-Sarah might work together for our mutual benefit and that of the city.

Since my discussion with Mr. Bannecker, I have thought a great deal about the possibility of Southwestern Bell participating with USEDC in a venture we are presently trying to get started. We are attempting to purchase the Lister building, located at the corner of Taylor and Olive, as part of our program to invest in the physical assets of the community. Before we can proceed with the purchase of this building, we must lease sufficient space to sustain our investment. Approximately one-third of the building is now leased and we estimate that we must lease one additional floor.

I have read of a new innovation in telephone service; the phone center. As I understand it, the telephone company installs jacks in apartment buildings, offices, university dormitories, etc., and new tenants pick up their phones at the phone center rather than having an installation man service each installation. There are plans for both housing projects and apartment buildings to be built in the west end and, of course, there are a large number of apartments in this area. In addition, the Lister building is located relatively near St. Louis University, Barnes Hospital, and the whole Lindell corridor which is earmarked for redevelopment. Then too, the Lister building would be ideal for training facilities for minority employees located in the Union-Sarah area, as well as having the possibility for use as business offices of one type or another.

I am enclosing an advertisement giving some preliminary information about the Lister building, along with an article which tells a little about our real estate activities. We know that Southwestern Bell has a continuing need for office space, and we feel confident that we can serve to satisfy some of those needs. I look forward to hearing from you, and hope that we can meet soon to discuss how we might together help alleviate some of the causes of blight in the city of St. Louis.

Very truly yours,

/s/ H. E. (Pete) Berndt, Director
Venture Formation and Management

The response from Mr. Shockley closed the correspondence; this exchange was typical of that with all other corporations.

R. R. Shockley
Vice President, Missouri-Illinois

May 1, 1973

Mr. H. E. Berndt, Director
Venture Formation and Management
Union Sarah Economic Development Corporation
4526 Olive Street
St. Louis, Missouri 63108

Dear Mr. Berndt:

I read with considerable interest your proposal of April 18 that Southwestern Bell lease office space in the Union Sarah Corporation's Lister Building. The idea you advance in your proposal is a good one. And your knowledge of our new Phone Center operation indicates that you have been thorough in your "homework."

However, our engineers have advised me that Southwestern Bell has no current requirements for office space in the city's west end. Nor do they anticipate a need for more space in the near future.

We will keep your proposal in mind, however. I have forwarded your letter to Bob Bannecker and he will keep it on file in the event that the current space situation would change.

I'm glad you were able to visit with Bob a few weeks ago.

Sincerely,

/s/ R. R. Shockley

In February 1973, shortly after the first contacts with Monsanto were initiated, USEDC met with its manager of Equal Opportunity Affairs. At this meeting, it was learned that Monsanto had been working with another community group to start an industrial laundry. If the project were started, the company would receive the business Monsanto was at that time giving to other laundries. The other community was having problems getting the project underway, and it was indicated that Monsanto would go with USEDC if USEDC could produce the facility. However, a feasibility study indicated that the project was not viable, and it was subsequently dropped on the recommendation of USEDC.

Our efforts at convincing major corporations to contribute to the community development program of USEDC proved unsuccessful. Corporations, in business for profit, wish to associate with community economic development corporations on a profitmaking basis. One such business relationship was established with Wetterau Corporation and the Union Sarah IGA supermarket.

The Union Sarah Community IGA opened on June 19, 1974, with a great deal of publicity and optimism. Special emphasis was placed on choosing a manager, as management is the most pressing problem in all subsidiary operations. The person finally hired had eighteen years experience in retail groceries, good references, and a reputation as hard-working entrepreneur. Arrangements were made with Wetterau Corporation to act as the wholesale distributor, provide management assistance, and supply the accounting functions. Every effort was made to build in all the safeguards and controls available.

The store was located in what had formerly been a Kroger store. The Kroger Company had closed the store because stores with areas less than 20,000 square feet find it difficult to move enough products to be profitable. With the employee wage rate demanded by unions, the wages as a percentage of gross income generally became too high. Thus, failing to turn a profit, Kroger decided to close the store.

USEDC staff did a feasibility study to determine whether the store could operate profitably. Kroger was doing between $20,000 and $25,000 gross business each week, and the consensus was that a community-owned store, if properly operated, could do as well. In an attempt to increase the gross and to keep wages down, the store would be operated on a nonunion basis and would open six and one-half days per week. An incentive plan was adopted to encourage teamwork and to increase commitment.

Another inducement for opening the store was a relatively low investment for that kind of operation. The proposal requested $156,600, $50,000 of which was for initial inventory, $48,000 for working capital, $20,000 for a deposit to IGA, and the remaining $38,600 for renovation, equipment, and other initial startup expenses. Kroger transferred all of its equipment to

USEDC for $1, so that only about $25,000 was needed for new equipment.

After ten weeks, an inventory was taken and a profit and loss statement was prepared: it showed a $50,000 loss. Initial sales were better than expected with $22,000 the first four and one-half days, $30,000 for the first full week, and $32,000 the second full week. Sales began to drop off slowly, but after eight weeks sales were at $168,164, which was only $1,800 less than originally projected. At least part of the store's problem was poor refrigeration, which resulted in some sales of bad meat and spoiled dairy products. No one expected a major loss, however, and the $50,000 loss revealed in the first statement came as a distinct surprise. After investigation, it was learned that the weekly sales items were never re-priced and that the store was completely underpriced.

Because of such flagrant mismanagement, the manager submitted his resignation. He was replaced by the assistant manager and USEDC venture personnel.

In the meantime, Wetterau removed USEDC from central billing. Central billing is a major part of the accounting program USEDC purchased from Wetterau, which places the payment of all major expenditures through their accounting department. It provides a control for absentee management because it removes the major handling of accounts from managerial responsibility. However, because of the low cash flow situation, Union Sarah IGA was removed from central billing and lost its advantages. The following notice was sent to all vendors advising them of Wetterau's decision:

ATTENTION: CREDIT DEPARTMENT

Gentlemen:

Effective August 25, 1974 and until further notice, we will not be responsible for the payment of any merchandise purchased by Union-Sarah IGA Store # 114, We sincerely regret the necessity for this action. Will notify you if there is a change in these instructions in the near future.

Yours truly,

WETTERAU FOOD SERVICES

Upon receipt of this notice, almost all vendors demanded immediate payment upon delivery of merchandise, and some required that payment be made by cashier's check. In-house accounting efforts were immediately increased and a full-time bookkeeper was hired to keep up with this work. The cost of Wetterau's accounting service remained the same, even though their service had decreased and the in-house effort was increased.

As conditions at IGA worsened, a Wetterau store counselor suggested that Wetterau discontinue service altogether because of the overall mismanagement. USEDC agreed that the facts of mismanagement were correct, but convinced Wetterau not to take such a drastic action yet. USEDC then began to work out its very large problems.

Under the new management, the management-related problems began to be corrected, but the cash flow situation continued to worsen, as did the low sales. Another $60,000 was invested in the store, some of the refrigeration equipment was improved or replaced, and the advertising effort was stepped up to recapture some of the lost customers. USEDC now felt that the store was sufficiently stabilized to warrant its return to central billing.

Wetterau management denied USEDC's request, ending their letter as follows: "Please feel free to secure another supplier if you are unhappy with our retail accounting charge or any other service we perform."

Next, USEDC sent a letter to the president of Wetterau, explaining its position and past experience with the company. They were then invited to meet with the Wetterau management, after which they were returned to central billing.

This example reflects the attitudes of business toward CDC-type programs. Their primary goal is profit, and they do not intend to jeopardize profits for the sake of social action. Wetterau realized that the Union Sarah IGA operated in a low-income area, was inexperienced in the retail grocery business, and was located where a large chain, Kroger Company, left because they were losing money.

One of the major fallacies of CDC legislation, as well as of the CDC advocates, is that corporations are willing to participate in joint ventures. The legislation was written as if corporations were fully aware of their part in CDC development efforts. Most corporations, however, are not even aware of the legislation, let alone are they willing to participate.

Corporations exist to maximize profits. This very fact mitigates against social responsibility, though many feel compelled to appear socially concerned, as do many private citizens. In fact, corporations are concerned with making profits, and executives with their career goals and self-preservation. Neither corporations nor individual executives believe that the problems of the ghetto are their responsibility. As one highly placed executive stated to me while I was employed by a major corporation, "I suppose those people need help, and I suppose someone should help them, but I wouldn't give them a goddamn dime."

Thus, their rhetoric notwithstanding, the private sector has done very little. With the exception of Ralston Purina, USEDC has not benefited substantially from the St. Louis corporations. The following lists the assistance given:

1. Ralston Purina provided a $20,000 grant and a $90,000 no-interest loan to Belle Lane Terrace.

2. Ralston Purina provided a $25,000 short-term, no-interest emergency loan to Quantum Plastics. The loan was repaid within thirty days.

3. Monsanto Company provided industrial painting contracts for Prolific Designs, Inc.

4. Monsanto provided some technical assistance to Prolific Designs.

5. McDonnell-Douglas provided some technical assistance to Prolific Designs.

6. Monsanto and McDonnell-Douglas each had a representative on the board of directors of Prolific Designs.

7. Gateway Bank and City Bank have at different times been represented on the USEDC board of directors.

8. A Sears and Roebuck store manager and assistant manager sat on subsidiary boards.

9. The Oldsmobile regional manager sat on a subsidiary board, as does a Carter Carburetor engineer, and the president of General Mortgage Company.

10. Kroger Company transferred equipment with a replacement value of about $75,000 to the Union Sarah IGA for $1. Of course, the equipment could not have been moved or sold, and was of no real value to Kroger.

As a result of a general failure to get private sector support, USEDC's overt effort has been discontinued. Certainly, efforts are still made to interest corporations, but a defined strategy and program no longer exists.

The president is active in community organizations as is any other chief executive, and through these contacts he attempts to create interest in USEDC.

PHYSICAL DEVELOPMENT STRATEGY

Nothing reflects the quality of life in a community more than its physical environment. A community of neat lawns, well-appointed homes, and bright, clean, well-stocked shopping areas represents affluence. A community with derelict housing, vacant housing and vacant lots, single-family dwellings converted into multi-family or rent-by-room units, trash-ridden streets and alleys, and obviously run down and poorly stocked shopping areas represents the direst kind of poverty. Overall, Union Sarah belongs to the latter category.

At the 1970 census, Union Sarah had a total of 12,629 dwelling units. Of these units, the City of St. Louis Workable Program,[8] a St. Louis Planning Commission document, indicates that 69 percent, or 8,714, are in poor condition, i.e., require major rehabilitation in order to bring them up to minimum acceptable property standards. The USEDC real estate department estimates that, since the 1970 census, 785 units have been demolished and 350 have been renovated, which leaves 7,579 to be either renovated or demolished.

In addition to the derelict housing, the shopping areas of Union Sarah are dominated by vacant shops, boarded-up stores, and generally marginal business efforts. The area has only one major department store, Sears, and one supermarket, National Foods.

Since 1969, USEDC has focused on improving the physical environment through developing a shopping center, rehabilitating structurally sound existing dwellings, and constructing new dwellings. But to date no dwellings have been renovated nor have any new ones been built, and the shopping center is still in the preliminary planning stages. The single physical development goal achieved is the renovation of the health center.

The community residents would welcome a shopping center, as adequate shopping facilities are not available in the Union Sarah area. However, shopping centers in the inner city have been found to be very tenuous in other cities; I know of no successful shopping center development in an inner-city location. At the Second Annual Conference of the Minority

Shopping Center Assistance Council, held at the Gramercy Hotel, Washington, D.C., in June 1974, Samuel Rosenfeld of Rosenfeld Realty Company, a man with thirty years experience in the shopping center business, was asked if he would consider developing a shopping center in the inner city. Mr. Rosenfeld stated that he would not because "I am concerned with making a profit, and I don't think that I can do this in the inner-city."

Nearly all shopping centers located in inner cities are in serious trouble. For example, North Philadelphia's Progress Plaza, Winston-Salem's Winston Improvement Company, Chicago's State-51st Street Medical and Shopping Center, and the Martin Luther King Plaza in Cleveland are experiencing severe problems. An article in *The Wall Street Journal* stated, "The cards are so stacked against black centers, in fact, that the International Council of Shopping Centers is abandoning a three-year effort to help get them started."[9]

The factors limiting the success of inner-city shopping centers include an inadequate market to support the business tenants, failure to get at least one key tenant, a square foot development cost prohibiting competitive leasing arrangements, poor access from major arteries, and lack of a skilled workforce.[10] For example, the management of Martin Luther King Plaza in Cleveland, unable to find a key tenant, opened their own supermarket and became their own key tenant. The plaza is designed as an indoor mall, with sixteen townhouse apartments on the roof—an ingenious idea but one that increased the construction cost beyond feasibility. The plaza is located in the center of the Hough Area, one of the country's poorest ghettos.

Feasibility studies have been made on five suggested shopping center locations within Union Sarah, and in each case the studies indicated a combination of the above-mentioned problems. The main problem is that key tenants do not want to locate in an area they consider risky, where the land acquisition and construction costs are too high, and, most importantly, where the area cannot support a shopping center without considerable help from shoppers outside the area.

Creating new or renovating housing has been USEDC's most frustrating problem. Because housing is so necessary for the area's survival, it has been a high priority in the community even before the existence of USEDC. Thus far, all USEDC development efforts have failed.

The first USEDC development effort, Belle Lane Terrace (and also the most important because it was a low-income housing project), failed to materialize. The project was all the more important because a neighborhood group, Belle Neighbors, incorporated as a not-for-profit corporation and originated the plans. They later chose USEDC as the developer. The project was a low-rent, 107-unit public project that was to be turned over to the St. Louis Housing Authority upon completion for project cost plus an estimated $50,000 profit.

In July 1970, USEDC, working with the interreligious Center for Urban Affairs, obtained a no-interest loan in the amount of $90,000 from Ralston Purina to purchase seventeen parcels of land comprising the site. Subsequently, USEDC acquired a no-interest loan of $21,150 from the Episcopal church and $37,800 from the Presbyterian church to raze thirteen buildings and pay architectural and engineering fees. But a freeze by the Housing and Urban Development Department continued and finally killed the project.

In April 1971, the Board of Aldermen of St. Louis declared a development area within Union Sarah blighted.[11] The USEDC staff then developed a proposal to build a middle-income apartment complex and redevelopment project. An investment of $11,000 was made to purchase 80 percent of the property in the proposed area, but USEDC was unable to get mortgage insurance. Plans for divesture of this property are presently being considered.

The most ambitious real estate undertaking is the rehabilitation of Sherwood Courts Apartments located on the southern edge of Union Sarah. These were once the most prestigious apartments in St. Louis, but they have been unoccupied for the past six years and are now derelict buildings. USEDC purchased the property for renovation, and developed a program that included the design, construction, and financing of the project. With a commitment from a consortium of four St. Louis banks for $600,000 and a guarantee from Opportunity Funding Corporation for $200,000, it appeared certain that USEDC would finally get into real estate development. The original package cost was much below the actual, and the project was held up for over two years. However, a new financial package was developed, and the project began in the summer of 1976. It is expected to be completed early in 1977.

The enthusiasm for real estate development projects is seen in an article that I wrote for the April 1973 issue of *The West End Word.* In this article, planned projects are viewed as if they existed in fact; this same tendency is a factor in almost all advocate studies on the CDC movement. At the time I wrote the article, no one on the USEDC staff doubted that the projects listed would be completed. These projects represented our major efforts, we were encouraged by the people with whom we were working, including architects, bankers, contractors, and government agencies, and we were seeking recognition as an established community force. The article is as follows:

For the past three years the Union-Sarah Economic Development Corporation (USEDC) has been quietly working toward the ownership and management of major investment properties within the Union-Sarah area. To this end, three subsidiary corporations have been formed within the real estate department: Union-Sarah Realty Investment Corporation, Union-Sarah Housing Corporation, and the Union-Sarah Redevelopment Corporation.

USEDC recognizes that property development is an imperative, if local business is to survive and if new business is to be attracted to the area. The total program is designed for profit and to improve the environment. It is also USEDC's declaration of its firm commitment, as well as its confidence, in the total area embracing Union-Sarah and the West End.

Progress has been slow but steady, and USEDC now owns a $400,000 health center on Delmar; a $45,000 property at 4754 Dr. Martin Luther King Drive—presently occupied by Mid-City Rentals, a retail tool rental company; and is the owner under contract of a once-prestigious central west end office building, and will be advertising for tenants within the month.

Future programs, all in the advanced stages of planning, will provide a total of 224 housing units for an investment of over four million dollars. The largest of these is a 107-unit turnkey development at Fairfax and Pendleton, for which groundbreaking is planned in July. There is also a 57-unit rehab of a stately Central West End apartment building. Finally, there is a 60-unit middle-income apartment project proposed for Euclid Avenue near Washington.

This last project is presently designated as the C-3 redevelopment
project, and is in an area declared blighted two years ago by the
St. Louis Board of Aldermen. USEDC's Director of Real Estate,
Paul Mittelstadt, expects to name the project officially within
the next 60 days and is looking for suggestions. Any suggested
names will be welcomed. The apartment rents will range from
$160 to $205 per month, and will be of a mix of one and two
bedroom garden and townhouse apartments. They will feature
patios, balconies, loft bedrooms, 17 foot ceilings in some apartments, central air, and a full security system with TV monitors.
This project will represent an investment of over one million
dollars to strengthen an already growing Euclid area.

Although there is some concern at HUD regarding the viability
of the central west end over the next 40 years, the length of
the proposed mortgage loan, USEDC has shown its strong confidence in the future of the area.

Pete Berndt

In a sense, this article is a capsule review of all of USEDC's real estate
efforts. Other than the health center, none of the projects has been carried
out, and all but Sherwood Courts have been closed out. In each case, the
problem has been arranging the financial package, obtaining mortgage
insurance, or getting the proper HUD or Housing Authority approvals.
Obviously, it takes more than enthusiasm, or even venture capital, to make
the ghetto bloom.

The renovation and sale of single-family units is made difficult by the
lack of available financing. The per unit cost for single-unit renovation is
higher than that of multi-unit renovation, but "red lining"[12] is the more
serious problem. Inner-city locations nationwide face the red lining problem, and the problem has been made even greater by the dearth of lending
institutions participating in FHA loans.[13]

USEDC staff researched the extent of red lining in St. Louis and found
that of twenty-nine institutions surveyed, twelve, or 41.3 percent, indicated
a different loan policy for the city from that of the county. Of those twelve
ten required higher down payments (e.g., 25 percent for the city versus 10
percent for the county), one would not grant home loans in the city but
would in the county, and one would not make home loans outside of an

all-white St. Louis City area. Of the remaining seventeen, whose policy is the same for the city or county, two have down payment requirements of between 25 percent and 40 percent, which is excessive for poor and middle-income buyers. Therefore, almost 50 percent of the institutions surveyed have policies that work against groups acquiring property.

In an attempt to facilitate mortgage financing for new or renovated homes in the inner city, an article was written for *The West End Word,* asking for support from the affluent residents of the west end. In keeping with the strategy of informing prestigious St. Louis leaders, the article was also mailed to our mailing list, along with the following article about a mortgage pool established for Bedford-Stuyvesant:

"Citibank and Bedford-Stuyvesant"

Citibank has been active in providing financial support and management advice to the Bedford-Stuyvesant Restoration Corporation virtually since its inception.

Probably Citibank's single most significant contribution has been its role in creating a $65 million mortgage pool for Bed-Stuy homeowners. To form the pool, George Moore, chairman of Citibank at the time, spearheaded the effort to get 80 New York financial institutions to pledge the $65 million. As part of the pool Citibank has so far extended 48 mortgage loans with a total value close to $1 million.

The bank has also lent $200,000 to eight businesses sponsored by the Bedford-Stuyvesant Restoration Corporation, has extended several construction loans and has directly given $120,000 in corporate contributions. Through its summer intern program Citibank has funded jobs for Bed-Stuy youths during the past two summers.

Technical advice has also been an important contribution. A Citibank subsidiary, FNCB Capital Corporation, helped to standardize the bookkeeping procedures of the Restoration Corporation's Economic Development Division. And a consumer education seminar for the corporation's staff workers, with tips on family budgeting, was developed by Citibank's Education and Training Department.

William I. Spencer, Citibank's president, provides ongoing
advice as a member of the board of the Bedford-Stuyvesant
D & S Corporation, which works to galvanize business support
behind efforts to develop the area. Says Spencer: "Our main
role has been one of helping people to help themselves. Business has a lot to give—and to gain—from assisting communities
like Bedford-Stuyvesant."

Our letter suggested the possibility of developing such a mortgage pool
for home loans in St. Louis, and we requested that the business and political
leaders on our list add their support for such a pool. The following are typical of the answers received from the St. Louis leadership:

Dear Pete:

I appreciate your sending me the newspaper clippings relative
to the practice of lending institutions in the St. Louis and
New York areas. They do give some food for thought.

Sincerely,

/s/ John F. McDonnell
Corporate Vice President
Finance & Planning

Dear Mr. Berndt:

Thank you for your letter of June 6th and enclosures. I find
them of considerable interest. It has been my strong belief
that private money is absolutely essential to improve housing in our community. Hopefully, Mayor Poelker will work
in this direction.

Sincerely yours,

Joseph L. Badaracco

Dear Mr. Berndt:

Your letter of June 5 to David R. Calhoun, Jr., Chairman of
the Board of St. Louis Union Trust Co., and Edwin S. Jones,
Chairman of the Board of First Union, Inc., concerning the

lending practices of City Bank of New York promoting home ownership, has been referred to me.

My Division has the responsibility for First National Bank in St. Louis' home lending program and the possibility of a "pool" of loanable funds has been discussed from time to time by both our bank and other banks in the St. Louis community.

I am personally acquainted with your Director, Paul F. Mittelstadt, and can assure you that we have a continuing policy of making home loan funds available in the inner-city on a case-by-case consideration. I will be most happy to meet with you to discuss this matter in detail at your convenience,

Sincerely,

/s/ T. Barton French

Because of such responses, our strategy to interest the St. Louis private sector was discontinued. USEDC is still attempting to win private sector support, but only through contacts through common interests rather than through an intensive information campaign.

Physical development is still USEDC's primary objective for the 1976-1977 plan. In the past, real estate development efforts have been designed to utilize HUD, FHA, or Missouri Authority programs, but future programs will depend more on venture capital and conventional loans. This will free development programs of restrictions resulting from the changing policies of agencies other than OEO.

CHANGING STRATEGIES

During 1969-1975, USEDC developed and submitted four proposals to OEO, each containing a plan for a two-year period. All four proposals planned projects in business and physical development, each plan reflecting slightly different strategies. The strategies were generally based on CDC ideology, OEO policy, and the past experience of the USEDC staff and board. More often than not, the practical applications were governed by the exigencies of community and business realities.

The proposal covering the first two-year period, June 1969 through May 1971, emphasized labor-intensive manufacturing efforts, a contractors' revolving loan fund, and the development of a shopping center. The results were strongly influenced by the then OEO emphasis on entrepreneurship and the community development ideology of black capitalism. Most of all, the outcome was determined by community resources. The physical limitations of the community prohibited labor-intensive manufacturing efforts.

The efforts of these first two years also complied with community realities. As mentioned earlier, a shopping center was found to be not feasible. However, the community itself, through a neighborhood group, Belle Neighbors, provided an important development possibility. The Belle Lane Project, although now abandoned, provided the corporation with good experience for future development efforts.

The second two years, June 1971 through May 1973, were largely shaped by the problem within existing ventures. The proposal called for extension of those ventures. The actual results were that more investment moneys were placed in PDI and Quantum to help them survive. Rather than expansion, attempts at different manufacturing techniques were made to find a product mix that would work. During this period, the emphasis was on stabilizing ventures that had been started; no new ones were initiated.

In the area of physical development, the building to house the health center was purchased and renovated. Although USEDC acted only as an enabler for the health center, the project was conceived by the community corporation; the health center remains USEDC's single most significant achievement.

In the third two-year period, from June 1973 through May 1975, a a proposal with a somewhat new strategy was made in the area of venture or business development. This strategy, too, was influenced by OEO's informal policy and the experience of the national CDC movement and USEDC. During this period, the thrust was on acquiring existing businesses and making joint ventures with large corporations or other stable business interests. In either mode, a management component was the raison d'être of the strategy as one way to assure adequate management. A condition of purchase for each acquisition was to be that existing management remain until new management was trained and the business stabilized. Joint venturing was to require the corporate partner to provide a management component on a one-to-one basis, until the venture was at a point of equilibrium, and a marketing umbrella, a protected market, to a breakeven point.

USEDC investigated the possibilities of a tire retread company, carburetor rebuilding company, lithographic blanket manufacturer, industrial laundry, fast food service, temporary employment service, and community supermarket. Of these, USEDC negotiated for the industrial laundry, lithographic blanket company, and fast food company as joint ventures. None of these materialized. The retread company and the carburetor rebuilding company were existing businesses. The retread company was rejected, but the carburetor rebuilding company became an established venture. Both the temporary employment service and the community supermarket were established and both are now defunct.

The temporary employment service, USTES, did reasonably well until the end of 1974 when temporary employment began to decline. The decline occurred after the service's three UYA students were no longer involved in its activities. The major reason for its failure, however, was undercapitalization, resulting in inadequate manning. A proposal was submitted to OEO requesting $30,000 in order to staff this venture properly and provide necessary working capital. OEO rejected the proposal and so USTES was closed.

In the case of Masco Products, an already established business, trouble centered on the manager. He was from the community, but he was inexperienced and had difficulty learning management skills. This factor, together with the complexities peculiar to the auto aftermarket and a decreasing market demand, resulted in a loss of more than $40,000 in the first year. A reduction in force has brought about some decrease in losses, but not enough to make the project viable. OEO indicated it would probably not approve a proposal for additional investment and so the idea has been abandoned.

Once again, the strategy put forth in this proposal was set aside in order to get something started. USEDC was unable to get the private sector interested in joint ventures, and the management component for the only acquisition, Masco Products, proved undependable. In the cases of all three of the ventures started in 1973 and 1974 (USTES, Masco, and Union Sarah IGA), inadequate management had serious consequences. All three ventures failed.

The inability to find competent management is a continuing problem, as is obvious in the example of Masco. If a CDC is to follow the ideology of the movement behind it, managers should be selected among community residents and be given training. Once managers are brought in from the out-

side, then a major stated objective of the CDC is set aside. To succeed and
compete, however, experienced management is needed. Thus, USEDC,
along with most other CDCs, must reach outside the community for management skills.

As stated earlier, the original proposal for the fourth two-year period
was not approved. The second proposal, covering the period January 1,
1976, through December 31, 1977, emphasizes physical development,
especially community housing, with only a minimal amount of business
development. Having been unsuccessful in developing new businesses,
USEDC will concentrate on acquisitions and joint ventures.

GOVERNMENT PARTICIPATION

The CDC is a federal program under OEO, and the federal government
acts as its major funding agency. CDC can also draw on a number of federal
programs for support, such as the Small Business Administration, Office of
Minority Business Enterprise, and Department of Commerce.

USEDC, as an OEO-sponsored program, of course, gets a major portion
of its assistance from OEO. OEO has provided some $4.6 million since 1969.
OEO also gives technical assistance and continuing advice. Since OEO
reviews every board-approved feasibility study before it gives approval,
a close relationship has existed between the CDC and OEO staff, particularly the analyst assigned to USEDC. The OEO staff is, in fact, the control-
ling factor in USEDC's investment decisions.

Since USEDC has not reached self-sufficiency, the ultimate control of
the corporation rests with OEO. At each funding phase, from the two-year
proposal funding through funding requests for specific investments, OEO
has the veto power. OEO also sets conditions when it approves grant
proposals and when it releases funds for investment.

A very good example of OEO staff control can be seen in its rejection
of the USTES proposal. Although USTES was well within OEO guidelines
that the businesses be socially beneficial, OEO rejected the request for
more funds. This decision reflects the present temper at OEO, which now
encourages only profit-maximizing projects.

Although USTES was approved by the USEDC board of directors and
staff, OEO refused approval. Thus, local control is only minimal and is
possible only after OEO approval and compliance with OEO conditions.

In other words, the CDCs are actually dependent agencies and have no real local authority.

OEO's staff actions during review visits greatly influence the board-staff relationship and decisions. During discussions, the OEO staff injects its own concerns and ideas about the CDC's direction; these ideas later emerge as either board or staff recommendations. Because of their inherent power of life or death over CDC activities, OEO staff opinions are often accepted as those of experts, when they are often no more than reactions to perceived problems based on a cursory knowledge of events.

In addition to OEO, the federal programs utilized by USEDC have been the Small Business Administration, Opportunity Funding Corporation, and ACTION. Several meetings have been held with officials of the Economic Development Administration, but none of them ever produced results.

ACTION has been of greatest assistance and has had the longest relationship with USEDC. The original USEDC staff was aided by VISTA workers, whose primary responsibilities were feasibility studies and financial analyses. The VISTA workers were replaced with University Year of Action students from the University of Missouri at St. Louis. These students have made up a large percentage of the Venture Department staff and have proven essential to the department. They have also performed in both the Administration and Real Estate departments. The precise contribution of ACTION to USEDC would be difficult indeed to measure.

The Small Business Administration has contributed by guaranteeing loans to USEDC subsidiaries, specifically Quantum Plastics and Prolific Designs, Inc. USEDC has also provided a loan packaging service to residents in cooperation with SBA.

The Opportunity Funding Corporation (OFC) was involved in the guarantee of $200,000 of a $600,000 loan committed to USEDC by four cooperating local banks for the rehabilitation of Sherwoood Courts Apartments. OFC's guarantee, in fact, persuaded the banks to participate. However, USEDC was unable to contract the project at the estimated cost and lost the banks' commitment. They are still trying to put together a viable package.

Participation by local and state governments has been almost nonexistent. Although contacted frequently, the local administration has taken little interest in a program that has brought over $4 million of development money into the community. Assistance by departments, such as the City Planning Commission, has been unsatisfactory. It appears that the

CDC is of little or no interest to the city government. An example is seen in USEDC's attempt to enlist the Planning Commission's cooperation in the initial planning of the proposed shopping center. It took over six months, several letters, many phone calls, and the intercession of the mayor's office to get the Planning Commission to write the supportive letter necessary as the first step in invoking Missouri Law 353 by the Board of Aldermen.

On the state level, the governor's office was very supportive in getting funds for the 1973 proposal released. An official from the governor's office traveled to Washington with the president of USEDC and interceded in the governor's name for the release of USEDC grant funds. There has been no other state involvement with USEDC.

Just as the private corporations seemed unaware that they had a defined part in the Special Impact Program, as spelled out in the original legislation, so too were the state and local government agencies unaware.

THE PROGRAM BENEFIT–COST

When considering the benefit-cost perspective of this program, several factors must be remembered. To begin with, it is a demonstration program, which means that it does not have the support of a fully accepted federal program. It is, so to speak, still trying to prove itself. Second, some of the supposed benefits do not lend themselves to any real measurement; e.g., community pride, better self-image, improved racial attitudes, and strengthened leadership characteristics among blacks. Third, the adequacy of funding must be weighed.

After all these factors are considered, it is still fair to look at the measurable results of jobs created, new or renovated housing completed, community assets assumed, and overall profitability. Indeed, if the CDC is to be an example of community capitalism, then the bottom line should be analyzed.

Aside from in-house corporations (sometimes referred to as "paper corporations" because they are facilitators and not employers), USEDC has only one operating corporation: Mid-City Rentals. Including USEDC staff, a total of twenty-two people are employed, five of whom are from the community. (See Table 9.) This figure is substantially less than the original proposal goal of 400 persons in two years, which was overly optimistic anyway. These jobs do not reflect the total impact on employment, however. In addition, the health center employs over one hundred people, and a considerable number of jobs were created by the Contractors' Revolving Fund. Exact statistical data are not available on the number of persons employed by the Fund.

A review of businesses that were successfully initiated indicates five corporate failures, and one operating marginally. The two revolving loan funds were less than successful—the Precision Tool fund ended with an $18,000 loss and the Contractors' Revolving Fund experienced a $59,000 loss. There has been no housing development, but the Real Estate Investment Corporation has invested $238,000 in property occupied by Mid-City Rentals and the health center and has committed another $210,000 for rehabilitation. The Mid-City and health center properties have produced profits of $110,900.

A legitimate question is whether the $4.6 million, if utilized differently, could have produced greater benefits. At this point, however, the question is academic. The important question is: "Was the quality of life for poor people improved?" Does a demonstration program of this nature have a co-opting effect on potential leadership, whose demands might otherwise be more productive, or has the program demonstrated that community development programs improve the quality of life for poor people, or can they improve it with higher funding levels? What investment would be necessary to effect change in the community at a level that would appreciably improve the conditions of the poor in the community? The experience of USEDC, at least, would indicate that there was no improvement in the quality of life. There are strong implications, however, that this result was not a factor of investment level, but rather of program philosophy and methodology.

Our review of Union Sarah Economic Development Corporation seems to indicate that the control of the corporation is vested only nominally in a small group of middle-income residents and to a greater extent in the staff, almost all of whom are nonresidents. Ultimate control, however, rests with the OEO staff in Washington, which makes the final determinations on the release of funds. If the CDC ever became independent of Washington but did not increase the residents' participation, control would center in the board and staff, much as in any other corporation. Simply stating that the opportunity for resident participation is available does not make it a fact.

The level of profitability possible would seem to make the question of community control moot. As we have seen, USEDC ventures have failed, or are marginal at best, and the level of profits necessary for both independent action and an improvement in the quality of life for the poor of Union Sarah seems beyond reasonable expectation.

Not only is USEDC not profitable, but its direct impact as a community employer is very small. Taking the USEDC staff and all operating ventures together, USEDC employs only five people from the community out of a total of twenty-two employees. Of these, only one, the corporation president, has a position of significant responsibility.

In the area of physical development, USEDC has successfully renovated the Union Sarah/Yeatman Health Center. This is a very significant accomplishment, as the health center employs 104 people, many of whom are residents; provides health care for community residents; and houses a senior citizens center and the offices of USEDC.

It is not surprising that USEDC has been unable to gain the private sector's support. Given the profit motive of American corporations, they cannot be expected to be involved in other than a profit-making way.

The important question concerning a case study is whether the case study reflects a unique instance or the general experiences of like organizations. Has USEDC failed because of poor management by the staff or because of defects in the model itself?

All indications are that the failure of USEDC rests with the model defects and basic assumptions of community economic development. While USEDC compares favorably with other CDCs, the only accurate way to determine if St. Louis is unique is to look at the experiences of other CDCs. Chapter 5 reviews and analyzes the other urban CDCs funded by the OEO.

NOTES

1. ABT Associates, Inc., *An Evaluation of the Special Impact Program* (Final Report) (Cambridge, Mass., December 1973), p. 352.

2. See Stewart E. Perry, "Black Institutions, Black Separation, and Ghetto Economic Development," *Human Organization* (Fall 1972); Geoffrey Faux, *CDCs: New Hope for the Inner City* (New York: The Twentieth Century Fund, 1971); Charles Hampden-Turner, *From Poverty to Dignity* (Garden City, N.Y.: Anchor Books, 1975).

3. USRIC is more profitable, but it is an in-house venture whose profits are derived primarily from ownership of the health center.

4. Civic Progress is an organization of business leaders said to be extremely influential in determining St. Louis's priorities. See Ernest Calloway, "Who Runs St. Louis and How," *The St. Louis American* (October 18, 1973).

5. *Congressional Record,* Senate, January 15, 1969, p. 833.

6. *New York Times,* June 21, 1968.

7. A thorough study of this project, as well as corporate social activities in St. Louis, is found in the following doctoral dissertation: Kenneth John Newbeck "Social Responsibility and the American Corporation: A Benefit-Cost Perspective," St. Louis, Washington University, 1972, p. 307.

8. *The Workable Program for Community Improvement* (St. Louis City Planning Commission, May 1974).

9. "Shattered Dreams: Black Leaders' Plans to Build Ghetto Stores Often End in Defeat," *The Wall Street Journal,* May 1, 1972.

10. An excellent source for a method of site evaluation is Victor Gruen and Larry Smith, *Shopping Towns, USA* (New York: Van Nostrand-Reinhold, 1960).

11. This program results from Missouri Blighting Law 353, which allows for eminent domain and tax benefit to developers.

12. A term used to describe practices of lending institutions and insurance companies to refuse loans and insurance at reasonable rates in specifically defined low-income areas.

13. *The Wall Street Journal,* May 14, 1973.

part 3

OTHER URBAN COMMUNITY DEVELOPMENT CORPORATIONS AND STUDY CONCLUSIONS

INTRODUCTION

A total perspective of the community development corporation concept would embrace not only the urban CDC, but the rural CDC and all supportive efforts as well. For the purposes of this study, no in-depth aspects need be investigated beyond concerns of the urban CDC. Chapter 5 will briefly review the progress of fourteen urban CDCs. The data for this review have been taken from an evaluation of the Special Impact Program by ABT Associates, Inc.[1]

The discussion is limited to urban CDCs because the scope and purpose of rural CDCs are different from those of the urban efforts. The rural CDC typically embraces large areas; for example, the Home Education Livelihood Program covers the state of New Mexico, and Delta Foundation covers fourteen counties in Kentucky. It would seem that these are better described as area development corporations than as community develop-

ment corporations. The urban CDC is concerned with discrete populations—
black, Chicano, etc.—within relatively small areas. The rural CDC, on the
other hand, involves a more heterogeneous population within a larger,
more varied area.[2] Also, area economic development typified by the rural
CDC became a reality long before the Special Impact Program came into
being.[3] The Tennessee Valley Authority, which covers seven states and
has existed for over three decades, is in a sense a development corporation
but does not fall within the scope of this study.

The urban CDC characteristically represents a relatively small geographic
area with a high-density population. The population is generally homogene-
ous, in most cases black, and has a large percentage of unemployed and un-
der-employed. Business in the area is mostly owned by nonresidents, with
the exception of some small efforts often termed *Mom and Pop*-type businesses, and much of the industry has either left the area or is trying to
leave. Housing in the urban areas is generally deteriorating or decayed, although there might be pockets of kept-up neighborhoods occupied by the
owners. This general state of decay causes a reduction of city services—
both quantity and quality—which in turn causes further urban decay and
outmigration of upwardly mobile people.

The target area also typically has a high crime rate and an inordinately
high unemployment rate among young people between eighteen and twenty-
five years of age. There is also a disproportionate number of older poor,
unable to move out and unable to bring about necessary changes in the
community. The community thus characterized reflects the general condition of urban areas designated as Special Impact Program areas.

In addition, the CDC movement includes CDCs supported by private
foundation grants or other means. These, too, are not included in this study,
because accurate data on them are not readily available and because they
do not result from legislation or national policy.

Two other efforts integral to the CDC movement are the Center for
Community Economic Development (CCED), and the National Congress
for Community Economic Development (NCCED). Both of these organizations provide an ideological dimension to the movement as well as efforts
in research, consultation, and lobbying. The CCED is funded almost entirely
by the OEO, and is a research effort that provides information and reports
on community economic development activities. It acts as an advocate for
the CDC concept and gives advice both to OEO for forming policy and to
the CDCs for planning and operations. CCED maintains a library concerned

with community economic development and publishes a monthly newsletter on CDC developments and activities. CCED also publishes staff studies on matters of importance to the CDC movement.

The NCCED previously received funding from a private foundation (the Clark Foundation) but is now supported almost entirely through an annual fee assessed each member organization. Its membership is made up of CDCs and its board of directors is chosen from this membership. NCCED attempts to form policy acceptable to the CDCs individually and as a whole in order to forward consensual programs and a united front. NCCED is the spokesman for the CDC movement.

In addition, a large number of consulting and auditing firms around the country are involved with CDCs and OEO. Annual OEO audits are done at the expense of the individual CDC by independent auditing firms chosen by the CDCs. There are many other consulting activities demanding the services of a number of firms, some of which depend heavily on the CDC movement for their existence. OEO also employs various consulting firms in activities related to the CDC movement.

NOTES

1. Unless otherwise noted, data cited in this chapter are from ABT Associates, Inc., *An Evaluation of the Special Impact Program* (Final Report) (Cambridge, Mass., December 1973).

2. Exceptions are efforts on Indian reservations, i.e., Lummi Tribal Enterprise and Impact Seven, Inc., although Impact Seven also includes white farming communities.

3. See W. Paul Brann, et al., *Community Economic Development Efforts: Five Case Studies* (New York: Committee for Economic Development, 1964); and Donald R. Gilmore, *Developing the Little Economies* (New York: Committee for Economic Development, 1960).

5

A PROFILE OF URBAN COMMUNITY DEVELOPMENT CORPORATIONS

The previous analysis was concerned specifically with Union Sarah Economic Development Corporation and its performance relating to such factors as community control, private sector participation, physical development, employment impact, profitability, and potential self-sufficiency. In all of these areas, USEDC has failed to demonstrate sufficient success, or even potential, to affect the quality of life for the poor. This chapter attempts a similar review of fourteen CDCs presently funded by OEO as part of the Special Impact Program: Bedford-Stuyvesant Restoration Corporation; Black Development Foundation of Buffalo, New York; Black Economic Union of Kansas City; The Circle, Inc., of Roxbury, Massachusetts; Denver Community Development Corporation; East Boston Community Development Corporation; East Central Citizens' Economic Development Corporation of Columbus, Ohio; Greater Memphis Urban Development Corporation;

Harlem Commonwealth Council; Hough Area Development Corporation of Cleveland, Ohio; Inner-City Business Improvement Forum of Detroit, Michigan; Mexican-American Unity Council of San Antonio, Texas; North Lawndale Development Corporation of Chicago; and the Peoples Development Corporation of Washington, D.C.

ABT Associates, Inc. was awarded a contract by OEO in July 1970 to do an evaluation of the Special Impact Program over a three-year period. The study was concluded in June 1973, and its Final Report was published in December 1973. The data developed in this report and two interim reports, twelve volumes of data and analysis, provided the basis for most of this chapter.

In some respects, the ABT study was biased. Its final report overstated some data and gave an impression of greater success or activity than actually existed. For example, in its section entitled "Number of Housing Units Planned or Completed," the ABT study indicated that USEDC had "planned or completed" 172 units. Actually, USEDC has not completed any housing. Similar exaggerations occur elsewhere, creating significant inaccurate impressions. On the other hand, the separate data for Bedford-Stuyvesant appear to be more reliable. Exact figures are presented, and statistics are divided into completed new construction, completed rehabilitation, new construction and rehabilitation to be completed in 1973, and planned new construction and rehabilitation. Such a format leaves fewer doubts as to what has actually been accomplished.

Apparent overstatements also appear in the section "Public and Private Sector Financial Support." The value of technical assistance for USEDC, and perhaps for other CDCs as well, is greatly inflated. In addition, loans received from lending institutions are included as part of the private sector's contribution to the CDC effort. This exaggerates the private sector's contribution, since these loans are generally fully guaranteed and have more than adequate collateral. In fact, the opposite is true. These loans represent a contribution to lending institutions from CDCs. Indeed, in its attempts to show how the disadvantaged benefit by the CDC movement, ABT seems oblivious to private sector and middle-class benefits. These weaknesses in the ABT Report do not appreciably affect our use of ABT data for this study. The data itself is substantially correct and these studies were the most comprehensive ever attempted. It is the ABT's use of the data, its interpretations that are defective. To the extent that the ABT report errs, it errs in favor of the CDCs.

Of the fourteen urban CDCs included in this chapter, the five largest, comprising 82 percent of the total funding value and about 85 percent of the total population, will be emphasized. These CDCs—Bedford-Stuyvesant, Harlem Commonwealth, Hough Development, North Lawndale, and Peoples Development—are the most important not only because of their large size but also because they reflect the philosophy and structure of the others.

COMMUNITY CONTROL IN URBAN CDCs

As pointed out earlier, OEO has final control over the CDCs. One factor that somewhat tempers that control, however, is that OEO is in turn limited by Congress, in that Congress must approve the budgets for all government departments. Therefore, CDC does have some political clout. Among all other CDCs, Bedford-Stuyvesant has the greatest political power, highest funding level, and largest population.

Bedford-Stuyvesant's political clout also reflects on where the real control lies. The board of Bedford-Stuyvesant Development and Services Corporation includes people such as Senator Jacob Javits, Mrs. Robert F. Kennedy, the chairman of Mobil Oil Company, and the president of the First National City Bank of New York. The board of the sister corporation, Bedford-Stuyvesant Restoration Corporation, is made up of twenty-one directors drawn from representatives of financial, union, religious, and municipal organizations, "along with several local citizens of repute who are in the main businessmen, attorneys, and professional people."[1] The two corporations act as one; in fact, there is only a single staff. Both boards, chartered in New York as membership corporations, involve members who can elect other members. All members are also directors.[2] Barry Stein considers Bedford-Stuyvesant an organization "internally controlled and self-perpetuating, with no formal power held outside the corporate membership group."[3] Stein also includes a demur by the staff of Bedford-Stuyvesant, which indicates that indeed the poor do not have a direct voice in the corporation but are represented by people whose intent is to benefit the poor.

It is not true to state that we are characterized by "self-perpetuating" internal control. Restoration is controlled by its Board of Directors, which is external to the corporation—it is made up of community residents. Our activities are further controlled by the laws of New York State (external), the statutes of New York City (external), and the policies and directives of OEO (external). Clearly, to stress this "internal control" point is to beg the question. A word is also in order on the question of "self-perpetuating" versus what? The problem with the "antipoverty" program to date has been the three-year tenures for the community members of the boards. This is seen by many as a sure road to failure, since by the time unsophisticated community residents begin to acquire some expertise and understand what the program is all about, they have to step down, to be replaced by an inexperienced board. This ensures that any such program will never come of age and will always remain dependent upon outside consultants and TA contractors under the guise of "experts."

Further, we feel the ultimate in accountability is to be around to either reap the benefits or suffer the consequences of one's decisions. A "self-perpetuating" board has to reap what it sows; a short-term board leaves a legacy of bad decisions for someone else to deal with. Only since the advent of the antipoverty programs and the concomitant mentality have "long-term commitment" and "continuity" become dirty words.[4]

This defense of a "self-perpetuating" board is certainly contrary to the ideology of the CDC movement, which encourages greater community participation so as to develop the confidence in participating residents which will eventually change their self-image. This is certainly in opposition to the advocate positions mentioned earlier espousing community control in order to enhance the rates of integration. Furthermore, the last sentence is a sure indication that the Bedford-Stuyvesant staff does not agree with these concepts.

Outside of the OEO staff, then, control rests with people of influence such as Senator Javits, important community businessmen, attorneys, and professionals, and the Restoration/S&D staff. The community does not control the corporations, especially not its poor.

If the staff is a significant control factor, particularly in the daily decision-making and in shaping board opinion, who are the staff? Are they representatives of the community? Of the poor? Before the staffs of the two corporations were merged, Bedford-Stuyvesant Development and Services Corporation had a staff of nine, headed by a former Justice Department assistant attorney general for civil rights. Other staff members had backgrounds in private industry, management, foundations, and the state executive. All were white and only two were living in Bedford-Stuyvesant. In the present staff, 36 percent of the managers and 5 percent of the nonmanagers are from the community. Hence, by any definition, community control is minimal.

The Harlem Commonwealth Council (HCC) represents a population of 360,000 people. HCC frankly emphasizes profit, a position that is reflected by both its board and staff makeup. "HCC's emphasis on venture profitability has led to a careful choice of board members who are involved in economic groups outside the CDC."[5] Thirty-eight percent of the managers and 50 percent of the nonmanagers reside in the area. With a total employment of 191, and with less than half of them from the community, there can be little community control through staff performance.

HCC is another example of the impracticality of those who would have us believe that the interaction of residents with outside corporate leaders promote integration. With a population of 360,000, less than one hundred residents are employed in any capacity and less than fifteen in any responsible position. How, then, could real benefits accrue to the community in the area of integration? Integration is not even a goal of this CDC, stated or otherwise.

Even in the area of beneficiaries, HCC does not seem committed to community residents. The emphasis is on profit. "HCC activities are strictly intended to make a profit. The CDC is not unaware of other SIP goals (e.g., employment, human development, etc.) but sees its role as being strictly an economic developer, leaving pursuit of social impacts to the large number of social agencies in the city of New York."[6]

Phase 1 of the ABT Report states that "the board seems to function strictly as a mechanism to supply political legitimacy and internal planning inputs." This suggests that the CDC staff has the greatest control at HCC. In a CCED study conducted between July 1972 and early 1973, nineteen executive directors of CDCs responded to the question: "In general, how much influence do you think the following groups or persons actually have in determining the policies and actions of the CDC?" The rank order was the CDC executive, CDC board, OEO, CDC professional staff, and the CDC executive committee.[7] The community was not included as a category, presumably because it was reflected in all other categories.

With only 58,000 people, the Hough area does not have the population of Bedford-Stuyvesant or Harlem. It has the second largest funding with $9,711,000, however, and was the second CDC initiated as an SIP area. The Hough Area Development Corporation (HADC) was influential in the evolution of the CDC movement, as both of its former executive directors, DeForest Brown and Franklin Anderson, have played important roles in CDC. DeForest Brown is presently on the staff of CCED; Franklin Anderson was on the board of the National Congress of Community Economic Development but is no longer connected with Hough or NCCED.

In reviewing HADC, the ABT Report points out that the corporation has an appointed board that is selected with neither direct nor indirect resident roles, and that the key CDC staff functions are performed by well-qualified nonresident professionals. A survey taken in the community by ABT in 1973 indicates that residents do not feel that HADC has given them increased influence in community affairs.

In the two other CDCs, North Lawndale Economic Development Corporation and the Peoples Development Corporation, there is generally the same general absence of community control. ABT characterized North Lawndale as having a low community control ranking; North Lawndale deliberately maintains a low community profile in order to avoid resident frustration. Only 11 percent of its managers are from the community.

The Peoples Development Corporation employs a total of thirty-four people, only 33 percent of whom are from the area and none of whom is a manager. The ABT Report states: "In spite of concern for community involvement, PDC has had no direct relationship with its community."

The pattern established by these five important urban CDCs is followed by the nine remaining smaller CDCs. Typically, the professional staff is almost always found outside the community, the boards are made up of business and professional people who most assuredly are not poor residents, and profit-making rather than labor-intensive ventures are emphasized.

Given this information, the advantages of community control touted by CDC advocates do not exist. The real facts appear to be that the CDCs realize that to compete with other businesses the rationale of business must be accepted. Maximization of profits dictates that employees be hired on the basis of their efficiency and not on their place of residence.

Barry Stein suggests that Bedford-Stuyvesant operates in much the same way as all other large corporations. That is, like other corporations, Bedford-Stuyvesant must be exploitative and demand high-quality performance. If it does not, it will not succeed as an economic development corporation and will not achieve self-sufficiency.

None of the CDCs is yet close to self-sufficiency; each is still under the final control of OEO.

DEVELOPMENT STRATEGIES

Although development strategies and program objectives differ somewhat from one CDC to another, there are only a limited number of alternatives open. In most cases, more than one development strategy is operational at any one time and there is a natural evolution that develops strategy changes in a continuum. For example, USEDC's announced strategy in their initial proposal was to develop labor-intensive manufacturing ventures. When conditions prohibited this type of development and OEO began to favor entrepreneural efforts within the framework of black capitalist concepts, the actual development strategy was changed to accommodate those imperatives. In addition, most, if not all, urban CDCs include physical development as an ongoing strategy, while at the same time placing a greater or lesser emphasis on the respective business development strategies.

As an example, let us consider the experiences of Bedford-Stuyvesant Restoration (BSR). BSR's stated operational strategy embraces three areas of concern: economic development, physical development, and area development/public services. Economic development has been strongly influenced by the concept of black capitalism and entrepreneurship. As a result, the major emphasis of this strategy has been on supporting local business through loans rather than through an equity position (although this, too, is done). BSR has attempted to entice private sector corporations to become involved in joint ventures or to locate in the area. BSR has not been truly successful in this objective, even though IBM has located a plant in this area. This is not a joint venture, but a wholly owned IBM subsidiary effort located in a building owned by and rented from BSR. No other corporations have been involved in this way and none are partners in joint ventures.

The economic development program is specifically concerned with industrial and business development through support of existing and new businesses and through encouraging established corporations to develop subsidiary efforts in Bedford-Stuyvesant. A business development loan fund offers loans to entrepreneurs to assist them in startup activities as well as to give them operating capital or to support expansion activities. A program for local entrepreneurs offers them technical assistance in management, marketing, and business planning as well as in more technical areas, when requested. BSR maintains a similar loan and technical service for the construction industry in order to promote minority contractors. In an effort to attract outside business, BSR established the industrial development fund which offers loan packaging, location planning, and assistance in obtaining tax abatements. Finally, its economic development program includes a comprehensive manpower program, which is a job development and placement effort. It includes recruitment services, referrals, counseling, and on-the-job training.

The second strategy area, physical development, is probably the most successful and best known of BSR activities. It is also in line with the area found to be most important on the resident questionnaires; i.e., housing. The physical development strategy involves a number of different programs and several BSR subsidiary corporations. The Restoration Development Corporation acts as the developer and oversees all development activities; BSR Construction is the CDCs' general contractor, does all general contracting for CDC developments, and bids on outside developments; the Restoration Funding Corporation is a mortgage pool that provides financing for the construction of one to four family residential units; and the Sheffield Rehabilitation Corporation manages all rehabilitation and redevelopment efforts. BSR also has a property management division that manages all BSR property and attempts to capture property management contracts from property owners located in Bedford-Stuyvesant and bordering areas. Other related housing activities include the home improvement program, which is a block-by-block renovation of housing exteriors; training of residents in construction work and counseling tenants on their rights; and a co-op housing program that helps tenants in apartment buildings organize cooperative ownership mechanisms. Finally, BSR is engaged in the development of the entire block surrounding the new Restoration Center. As is the case nationally, BSR recognizes physical development to be the most viable vehicle through which the corporation can control community assets.

The third area of concern, the social programs area, includes the development of public services. These services are coordinated through community centers located in five areas of Bedford-Stuyvesant and address a number of community needs in health care, education, day care, and ex-offender programs. The most outstanding and best known effort to develop public services was the building of the Billie Holliday Theatre, through a grant from the Astor Foundation. In addition to its use as a professional theatre, it is also used by community organizations to hold fund-raising programs. (As stated earlier, the ABT Report does not make an adequate distinction between operable and planned projects; thus, a great portion of the above, particularly in the physical development area, represents projects that have yet to become reality.)

BSR has financial support from OEO and other sources that is equal to or greater than that of all other CDCs combined. At the time of the ABT Final Report in June 1973, BSR had received $31.7 million from OEO, $12.5 million from foundations, including $3.5 million from the Ford Foundation, $1 million from corporations, and $9.9 million from local banks. These figures include loans and in-kind services as well as grants.

Through its business and physical development efforts, Bedford-Stuyvesant has created visible achievements for the community. In the area of economic development, in 1973 through loan or equity it supported fifty-three businesses; ten manufacturing companies; seventeen retail or whole-sale stores; fifteen service-centered ventures; and eleven construction companies. The total employment resulting from these efforts was 557. In physical construction, the home improvement program has made significant progress. Involvement with this program is on the block level; at least 50 percent of the owner-occupied homes agree to pay $50 per house and to match the money BSR spends on the outside with cash or in-kind service improvements for the inside. Ten blocks per year are renovated, and there is a long waiting list of blocks waiting their turn. In addition, rehabilitation and new-home construction programs are underway.

BSR serves one of the nation's largest depressed areas, with boundaries including 653 square blocks and a population reported by ABT to be 301,380 but set forth by both the Ford Foundation and a CCED profile to be in excess of 450,000.[8] These statistics must be kept in mind in order to place BSR's achievements in proper perspective. With a population of around 400,000 people, BSR has created about 547 jobs through its fifty-three ventures and about 236 jobs in the CDC itself. Since only 36 percent of the managers and 54 percent of the nonmanagers reside in Bedford-Stuyvesant, only about 300 of these jobs were for residents. BSR also claims it has created a great many indirect jobs through its efforts, but these claims are somewhat questionable and difficult to prove or disprove.

Five thousand jobs are claimed as a result of the BSR manpower program and 500 more as a result of construction subcontracting. Since the permanence of these positions is doubtful, the benefits accruing to the community are difficult to measure.

Harlem Commonwealth Council has the second largest target population with 360,000 people, most of whom are blacks. It is located in the largest and most famous black community, which already boasts a strong institutional base. Harlem has a large number of social agencies that are privately, federally, state-, and city-operated. As a result, HCC's strategy is strictly oriented to venture profitability, without consideration of social benefits. This emphasis demands that board members be chosen for their business acumen and for their involvement with outside economic groups. Notwithstanding this business orientation, HCC has had no greater economic success than the other CDCs. At the time of data collection, only one of HCC's ventures, Acme Foundry, was even marginally profitable.

HCC has not focused on property development and therefore has neither planned nor completed any housing units. However, through its subsidiary, Commonwealth Diversified, Inc., it holds title to a seven-story, $8 million office building on Harlem's main thoroughfare, West 125th Street. The building houses HCC as well as city agencies, small businesses, franchise firms, and another subsidiary of HCC, Commonwealth Tours. According to the ABT Report, this holding produces an annual rental income of $190,000.

More than anything else, HCC is a government-subsidized holding company, doing business like any other business. HCC has had little contact with the community, employs its managers on the basis of ability only, and concerns itself only with profitability.

Hough Area Development Corporation is one of the oldest CDCs, having received initial funding in 1968. It is also one of the best funded CDCs, with funding through fiscal 1974 of over $9 million. HADC is located in a large black Cleveland community which is one of the most depressed urban areas in the country. During the urban riots of 1968, the Hough area attracted national attention. HADC was started in 1968 with initial SIP funding, its basic organization was formed in 1967 by a group of black community leaders called "The Machine." This leadership was drawn from those who had experience in civil rights, political, and antipoverty programs. Their objectives included community ownership and control of local businesses, development of commercial and residential property, and individual benefits for residents resulting from increased employment and other economic support. Their strategy included venture development in manufacturing, service, retail, and construction, assistance to entrepreneurs through loans and technical assistance, training, improved housing for residents, and improved consumer benefits resulting from HADC ownership of businesses.

HADC has developed a rubber manufacturing company, Community Products, Inc., Handyman Maintenance, and Hough Federal Credit Union as service corporations; two fast food outlets, McDonald's at 83rd Street and McDonald's at 107th Street; Homes for Hough; and Martin Luther King Plaza with the Top Value Food Market as its key tenant. None of these projects has done well; the only projects that are still viable are McDonald's at 83rd Street, Community Products, Inc., Homes for Hough, and the Top Value Food Market. Of these, HADC is planning to divest itself of the 83rd Street McDonald's and Top Value, neither of which has been profitable. Community Products, Inc., is holding its own at this time, although its losses are above $700,000.

In property development, Homes for Hough has created twenty-six housing units. HADC's greatest housing impact has been through its assistance to other property development programs through which over 600 new units and 1,000 units of rehabilitation have been developed. The other major real estate development, Martin Luther King Plaza, built at a cost of $3.5 million, is having difficulty getting off the ground. Unable to attract a key tenant, HADC started its own supermarket, Top Value Food Market, and became its own key tenant. That, and the fact that the Hough area is a low-income area that would have a problem supporting a shopping plaza, mitigate against the success of this project.

North Lawndale Development Corporation (NLEDC), funded since June 1969, serves a largely black population of 250,000 in the North Lawndale section of Chicago. The primary goal of the CDC is physical redevelopment of the target area; therefore a shopping center and industrial park are their two major endeavors. Their strategy is exclusively geared to creating economic benefits through the development of these two projects.

At the time of data collection, NLEDC had made no significant advance in providing community benefits. Its objective is to generate large private and public investments as leverage for SIP funds for long-term community benefits through property development.

The Peoples Development Corporation (PDC) in Washington, D.C.

received funding in June 1969 through its sponsoring nonprofit agent, the Peoples Involvement Corporation (PIC). PDC is the economic development arm of PIC, and its target area is the northwestern section of Washington which has a population of over 130,000, mostly blacks.

PDC is business-oriented, which is reflected in the fact that a high percentage of the staff has business experience. As a result, PDC has had a goal of high profitability probability rather than immediate community benefits. Nevertheless, Zebra Graphics, one of two PDC projects, is losing money. The other project, Murph's Hotel Corporation, offers the possibility of two hundred jobs and a high annual return on the CDC investment. At the time of data collection, the hotel project was not yet a reality.

In most cases, the urban CDC strategy embraces the philosophy of business; i.e., the development of ventures to provide a profitable base upon which to build. Venture success is definitely more important than individual benefits, at least in the short term. Almost all of the CDCs are striving for self-sufficiency within a foreseeable timeframe, five to ten years. However, at this point no CDC could sustain its operations over time without continued funding.

PRIVATE SECTOR INVOLVEMENT

As noted before, the I-D amendment stated that CDCs were "to unite the resources, expertise, and energy of American private enterprise with those of the public sector in a special attack on the problems of the nation's urban areas having the largest concentrations of poverty."[9] But, as pointed out earlier, USEDC was unable to obtain any but the most meager support from the private sector, even with a sustained program to attract support. Other CDCs attempted to attract private enterprise support and, for the most part, had the same experience as USEDC.

In almost every instance, the ABT study indicates that private sector participation on the CDC's board either is considered essential or is established to some degree. The overall conclusion is that the greatest amount of private sector participation is of this type, with technical assistance as a strong second. This use of the board and technical assistance to encourage investment participation has largely been unsuccessful.

The largest involvement of the private sector beyond that of advisors is that of lending institutions. The urban CDCs in this study were able to leverage $7,735,600 from private sector sources.[10] The vast majority of loans, however, were either 90 percent loan-guarantee SBA loans or loans to subsidiary efforts guaranteed by the CDC. These loans invariably have excellent collateral and provide a good return through interest to the lender. Lending institutions benefit significantly through their participation.

There is little evidence of private sector involvement in joint ventures, protected markets, or simply the location of plants in the CDC areas. Immediately following the civil disturbances of 1967-1968, a number of ghetto experiments were conducted by such firms as General Electric, Xerox, Boise Cascade, and IBM, but enthusiasm was transitory. The ABT Report states that "the brief and active corporate support of new subsidiaries or joint ventures in depressed areas convinced participants as well as observers that the rules of the game are the same no matter what the social overtones might be. Furthermore, the inherent costs of disadvantaged area investments make the effort impractical without government subsidization."[11] IBM's much-publicized effort in Bedford-Stuyvesant resulted from the participation of IBM's chairman, Thomas J. Watson, on the Bedford-Stuyvesant board. Barry Stein states:

> The decision to invest in the area was therefore partly a reflection of his [Watson's] interest and his willingness to do something, as well as a sign of good faith that it could be done well. Nevertheless, it has taken IBM a couple of years to develop the facilities to the present point, and it may be that the presumed additional cost, above and beyond that which a similar plant elsewhere would have required, has mitigated against the likelihood that other corporations would locate there.[12]

In the *Harvard Business Review,* David B. McCall, one of the original directors of the New York Urban Coalition, insists that it is nothing more than a "grand delusion" to think that social problems will be solved by business leaders without the incentive of the profit motive. He points out that New York's Urban Coalition had the cream of American business, including such leaders as David Rockefeller and Tom Watson, and that after six years virtually nothing of consequence was accomplished.[13]

It seems obvious that unless the economic system of the country is changed, or unless, at the very least, the rationale of the American corporation is changed, social problems will not be solved by the involvement of corporations.

A number of benefits claimed for CDCs, as was mentioned in Chapter 4, simply cannot be measured. Even if one grants the CDC advocates' position that the movement produces community pride, an improved self-image, and leadership, still, tangible results such as jobs created, houses built or renovated, and dependency value reduced must be expected. Only these can serve as indicators of change or improvement in the communities.

The following ABT Report data are for the Bedford-Stuyvesant area; next are given summary data for the other thirteen CDCs. Bedford-Stuyvesant is listed separately because its project is larger than that of the thirteen CDCs combined.

Age at time of data collection	67 months
Funding as of end of fiscal 1972	$30,684,000
Private sector dollars leveraged	$23,478,700
Public sector dollars leveraged	$1,798,800
Employment:	
Venture	547
CDC	236
Total	783
Reduced dependence	0
Employees receiving public assistance:	
Before CDC/venture job	2
After CDC/venture job	2
Percent of managers from area	36%
Percent of nonmanagers from area	54%
Housing (new construction):	
Completed	52
Planned	1,206
Housing (rehabilitation):	
Completed	55
Planned	486

Without wishing to diminish the potential impact of BSR, it should be noted that there is apparently no direct benefit to the poor from employment. Only about 40 percent of those employed, or 293, are residents of

Bedford-Stuyvesant, and there is no change whatever in dependence, that is, the number of people on public assistance affected.

The following is a summary data profile of the other urban CDCs in this study:

Average age at time of data collection	31 months
Total of all funding	$37,566,000
Total private sector dollars leveraged	$7,735,600
Total public sector dollars leveraged	$7,233,000
Total employment:	
Ventures	516
CDCs	165
Total	681
Total reduced dependency value	$28,000
Total employees receiving public assistance:	
Before CDC/venture job	37
After CDC/venture job	30
Average percent of managers from area	28%
Average percent of nonmanagers from area	60%
Total housing planned or completed	182

If one were to assume a population of about 2 million for the thirteen CDC target areas, the above funding level of $37,566,000 amounts to just over $7 per person per year. Even if the benefits are assumed to accrue over time from institution building, it would seem a meager investment indeed for the benefit of the nation's poor.

In the area of employment, taking into consideration that Bedford-Stuyvesant has a population of over 400,000 and the other thirteen CDCs, an estimated 2 million, the impact would seem very small. At the time of data collection, Bedford-Stuyvesant employed only an estimated 293 residents, an amount that had no effect at all on reduced dependency. The other CDCs had much the same experience, although they did have some small reductions in welfare.

Even in the area of housing, which is the area of Bedford-Stuyvesant's strongest impact, only fifty-two new units were constructed and fifty-five were renovated. The completion number for the other CDCs is unknown; 182 were planned or completed.

Both tabulations given above indicate that a very small portion of residents hold responsible positions, and even the total employed is relatively small. The impact in terms of community control and effect on integration would seem to be small indeed.

It can be concluded that the more extensive analysis of USEDC reflects the general experience of the community development management and that the conclusions by applying the research model to USEDC's experiences apply to the total CDC movement as well.

This analysis of community development corporations provides ample evidence that emphasis is being placed on venture development and, therefore, on the profit motive. It is assumed that ventures will provide employment for the target area, give residents a chance to participate in community decisions through membership on boards of directors, and produce profits that the community can reinvest or use for socially beneficial activities. The limiting factor is profit, without which nothing else is possible on a continuing basis. Therefore, the reason for the existence of the CDC becomes one of profit rather than one directly beneficial to the target area residents, and the way the CDC operates is much the same as in all other corporations. People are employed on the basis of their skills rather than their need for employment, and low-skilled personnel are exploited through the same hierarchical structures and reward systems prevalent in corporations. For example, in the USEDC's supermarket, employees were encouraged not to join the union and were paid less than union wages. As Robert Allen states in a discussion of black economic cooperatives: "even if a cooperative economic venture were successfully initiated, its managers, in order to keep it afloat, would have to be responsive to the demands and constraints imposed by the overall competitive economic system rather than the needs of the surrounding black community."[14]

Allen discusses the ghettos of the United States within a framework of neocolonialism and indicates that black capitalists are in the same position as native elites who cooperate with former enemies to control the colony.[15] He says that the only difference is that whereas whites once oppressed the ghetto alone, now the whites have the cooperation of an elite band of black managers and professionals. "Increasingly, the majority of the black population will find itself dominated by a new oppressor class, black instead of white."[16] These black capitalists aspire to be the new rulers of the ghetto. In a real sense, if the CDCs had been successful in their profit-making programs, then the staffs and boards of the CDCs might have emerged as the core source of these new rulers.

Since the CDCs have accepted the rationale of the corporation within capitalist society, it is not surprising that CDCs are also joining the institutions created to extend and consolidate corporate power. Individual CDCs are joining the Chambers of Commerce and local professional societies, while the National Congress of Community Economic Development has become a member of the National Association of Manufacturers and is developing a special membership opportunity for individual CDCs. These efforts are presumably being made to afford CDCs opportunities to attract assistance and cooperation from the private sector; at the same time, there can be no doubt that the CCDs have adopted the philosophy of corporations. It is not uncommon to hear a CDC manager state that "we are here to make a profit just like any other business." CCDs also are ruled by the same constraints that rule other corporations: to produce as cheaply as possible (exploitation of the worker) and to sell at a price as high as possible (exploitation of the consumer). The result of this acceptance is brought sharply into focus by the following statement from the Westinghouse Evaluation:

> Despite the lack of tangible change in Hough, the area appears to be one of decreasing community tension. HADC seems to be playing some part in fostering this trend by prompting on visible symbols of community control and by helping to hook Hough into parts of the outside power structure that were formerly closed to it. The acquiescence of the HADC leaders in the "system" they have always believed hostile is itself significant.[17]

Not unlike the large corporation, the CDC has become "a creation in the service of its own bureaucracy" and "serves the purposes of its own management."[18] Its raison d'être has become the maximization of profits because its survival is governed by the marketplace.

NOTES

1. Barry Stein, *Rebuilding Bedford-Stuyvesant* (Cambridge, Mass.: Center for Community Economic Development, 1975), p. 5.
2. Ibid., p. 4.
3. Ibid.
4. Ibid., pp. 4 and 5.

5. ABT Report, Final, p. 134.

6. ABT Report, Interim, p. 12-1.

7. Rita Mae Kelly, *The Executive Directors of CDCs* (Cambridge, Mass.: Center for Community Economic Development, 1974), p. 21.

8. A Ford Foundation Policy Paper, *Community Development Corporation: A Strategy for Depressed Urban and Rural Areas* (New York: The Ford Foundation, 1973), and Center for Community Economic Development Newsletter, "Profile: Bedford-Stuyvesant" (December 1973).

9. ABT Report, Interim, Vol. 2, op. cit., p. 6-1. Taken from Westinghouse Learning Corporation, *Evaluation of the Special Impact Program,* Vol. 1, p. 17.

10. Bedford-Stuyvesant is excluded, as it alone leveraged $23,478,700.

11. ABT Report, Interim, op. cit., pp. 6-19.

12. Stein, op. cit., p. 11.

13. David B. McCall, "Profit: Spur for Solving Social Ills," *Harvard Business Review* (May-June 1973): 46-47.

14. Robert L. Allen, *Black Awakening in Capitalist America* (New York: Doubleday and Co., Inc., 1969), p. 53.

15. Ibid., p. 65.

16. Ibid., p. 245.

17. Westinghouse Learning Corporation, op. cit., p. VI.

18. John Kenneth Galbraith, "What Comes After General Motors?" *The New Republic,* November 2, 1974.

6
ANALYSIS, CONCLUSIONS, AND CDC FUTURE

While the focus of this work has been on the CDC concept, poverty has been the main concern. Only if CDC changes the prevailing attitudes toward the poor and only if the conditions of the poor are improved can one justify continuance of the program. It is not enough that CDCs create a job, 100 jobs, or even 1,000 jobs. Nor would it be enough if they were responsible for the building of 10,000 dwelling units. If the condition of the poor remains unaffected, the program is simply not viable.

Until 1932 when Franklin Roosevelt was elected president, the U.S. government had evaded any responsibility for the care of the poor; the lone exception was the Freedmen's Bureau. The poor had to depend on local charity, and assistance was provided, for the most part, only to the "worthy" poor—widows, orphans, and the disabled. The able-bodied were expected to care for themselves and their families, in the true tradition of economic individualism. At the time of the depression, private charity was the sole recourse for the destitute in many places. But the massive unemployment and social problems produced by the depression made these local efforts increasingly inoperative. Federal assistance had to be developed. It came in the form of the National Recovery Act, a program designed within the framework of self-help, whose objectives were "to put more people to work, to give them more buying power, to insure just rewards for both capital and labor in sound business enterprise, by eliminating unfair competition."[1] Its major purpose was business recovery, however, not assistance for poor people.

Once the federal government entered the field of social welfare, it was never able to extricate itself and return to the tradition of local charity. But long-held beliefs and attitudes about the poor, notably that they themselves are responsible for their condition, die hard, and so programs have not been designed for direct relief. The most humane approach has always been to provide programs of self-help or programs that can change the character of the poor through education. The CDC movement is well within this latter tradition.

With regard to the CDC concept and its practical effects on the alleviation of poverty, the following conclusions may be stated. The results of the case study in relation to community control indicate clearly that the poor participate only minimally, if at all, at any level in the corporation. In fact, even the general community population is only minimally involved. They have achieved indirect involvement by their ability to vote for the community corporation board that controls the USEDC board. But few take advantage of even this indirect participation. Available data indicate that only about 10 percent of the population voted in the elections and even this low figure may be an overstatement. The president of USEDC is a resident and has the most authority and power, but other decision-making positions are filled by people from the outside. Only one-third of the staff are residents, and none except the president occupies an important position. Although a high proportion of the board are residents (88 percent), few can be classed as poor or representing the poor, and even fewer participate in an influential way. Since participation does not really exist, it must be concluded that community control is nonexistent. Thus, the projected results of community control—an improved community and self-image, the advancement of integration, and resident upward mobility—obviously have not occurred. And, too, as there have been no profits, no reinvestment has been possible.

The above is true not just of USEDC, but of all other urban CDCs as well. In all the other CDCs included in this work, outside specialists occupy most of the decision-making positions and boards of directors are strongly influenced by outside people. The community people who are participating represent middle-class values and interests, and not the poor. Barry Stein has indicated that Bedford-Stuyvesant operates much like General Motors.[2] The same might be said of all the CDCs included here. The major difference is that, in contrast to GM, none of the CDCs has been profitable.

In the final analysis, CDCs are controlled by the OEO staff, which has the authority over refunding and the release of already funded money for specific investments, and can (and does) impose special conditions on the approvals. Since no CDC is even close to self-sufficiency, control remains with the OEO staff; hence, all the rhetoric concerning the supposed benefits of community control is of little value and, even worse, misleading. Hampden-Turner's projected benefits repeat the exaggerated expectations of earlier advocates and have no substance in reality.

Another important consideration related to the question of community control is the development potential within these urban areas. Advocates speak as if there are vast assets for development, the control of which will move the poor up, at the very least, to middle-class status. In fact, these communities contain mostly liabilities and are now being abandoned. The question that must be faced is as follows: if established business and industry cannot make it in the inner cities, how can inexperienced poor people make it? All of the minuses of these locations that caused business interests to move out still exist. Add to these minuses inexperienced management and you have all the ingredients for failure.

The strategies that the CDCs have used for development of the target areas include the entrepreneural, the physical development, and the joint venture strategies. The entrepreneural strategy is very closely related to ideas of black capitalism and is also important to the concept of community control. Since a large number of existing community businesses are small retail efforts or light manufacturing, they lend themselves to entrepreneurship more than to corporate acquisition. Further, it is believed that the equity position of the entrepreneur encourages a greater effort and therefore facilitates success.

An entrepreneural effort can be successful when the entrepreneur has had previous management experience in the particular business involved, when a sustaining market is available, and when customers have confidence in the entrepreneur—in short, when all the necessary ingredients for success are present.

Given the environment of the target areas, the ingredients for success are seldom present. Many of the entrepreneural efforts have resulted from acquisitions of marginal businesses. These businesses often remain viable only because of the original owners' years of experience and hard work. The recently launched community entrepreneur seldom has that same level of experience, and as shown here, management inadequacies have greatly contributed to the failures and potential future failures of USEDC. Small businesses in the United States, wherever they are located, have a failure rate of better than seven out of ten,[3] but a ghetto business has even a greater struggle for survival. The future is yet more tenuous because in a recession black-owned firms are hit harder, crime rises still higher, and the concomitant increases in ghetto business costs are greater. In other words, the already depleted ghetto assets are reduced even more by unemployment, which causes an increase in crime, which causes increased costs. The recession cuts disproportionately into business depending on the local market; manufacturing is most vulnerable to cutbacks by their buyers.

Another major strategy for CDCs is physical development. The most successful CDC in this area is Bedford-Stuyvesant, which has physical development as its major development strategy. Physical development is used to provide employment, improve the community visually, return investments through rents and unit sales, and add support to their development corporation, property management corporation, and construction corporation, all of which attempt to function for profit on the open market. Physical development is also used to inspire pride and encourage cohesiveness through the neighborhood restoration program. After sixty-seven months of operation, Bedford-Stuyvesant had completed fifty-two new homes, with over one thousand more planned; fifty-five houses had been rehabilitated, with almost five hundred more planned; and their corporate offices, Sheffield Center, had been renovated and occupied. Although this record is very impressive when compared to that of all other CDCs combined, it is less so when one considers that more than 400,000 people reside in Bedford-Stuyvesant and that the area comprises an area greater than six square miles. None of the physical development corporations is profitable, and it is doubtful that they ever will be. Thus, these are basically subsidized developments and are not economically viable investments.

The thirteen other CDCs covered in the study have not been as successful. The ABT Report indicates that 182 houses have been planned or completed, but since this statement tells little about actual success, it is difficult to assess their progress. Even if all 182 houses were completed, considering that, combined, the thirteen CDCs represent over 500,000 people, not much success would be reflected. USEDC has completed no houses, either new or renovated ones; its single achievement has been the renovation of the building housing the health center, senior citizens center, and corporate offices.

These urban locations have a number of shopping centers, but none is profitable. The failure of the shopping centers highlights the reasons for the overall physical development failures: the shopping centers have been unable to get key tenants, their costs for property acquisition and construction have been too high to keep the square foot leasing costs in line with competition, and the market being served has not had a sufficiently high income level to support a shopping center.

In the case of new and renovated housing, much the same is true. People do not have the income to pay rents high enough to make real estate renovation profitable. New houses do not sell because lending institutions have red lined the areas, and savings are not high enough for large downpayments. In addition to other problems, many of the HUD-sponsored programs for inner-city projects have never materialized, mainly because of deficiencies in feasibility and financing. As a consequence, some programs, such as Belle Lane Terrace in Union Sarah, have had to be abandoned. The lack of financing and the red lining of certain areas in cities across the country relates to the total problem of private sector involvement.

The private sector was to play an important role in the CDC movement, for it was (and is) generally assumed to be needed for CDC success. But corporations have not been willing to participate at a level necessary to significantly affect the success of CDCs. The two most desirable ways for corporations to become involved are through joint ventures and through the location of labor-intensive plants in the areas. Past experience shows that neither effort can be expected. Facilities in the ghettos are not adequate for efficient operations, and new plants are too costly to construct in those areas becuase of land acquisition and demolition costs. Other factor such as lack of rail facilities, high insurance rates, high crime, an untrained workforce, and general disinclination by the corporations mitigate against both joint venturing and plant location possibilities. The private sector has demonstrated a real lack of interest in the needs of USEDC and of the other urban CDCs.

Basically, the private sector has been involved only in a limited way because participation would be contrary to their primary reason for existence—increased profits. Therefore, from a business point of view, their becoming involved would be irrational. Everything in the ghetto is opposed to the profit interest.

Over the years, the staffs of the CDCs have themselves come to understand why the private sector is not interested. As they have discovered, training residents to take over as managers does not give them the experience necessary to make the business a success, and merely telling residents that a store or other business is theirs is no guarantee that they will patronize the store. Nor does community ownership lessen vandalism or shoplifting when people are poor, angry, and without work. All the negative factors that have caused the failure of white-owned inner-city businesses are still there when the CDC takes over.

Taken individually or together, the CDCs discussed are not making profits for reinvestment in the community or for use to create socially beneficial programs. The CDCs have made very little impact on employment, and they have not even begun to affect the physical makeup of the communities served. In the case of USEDC, it has experienced a loss of over $500,000. With a total expenditure, venture and administrative, of nearly $2.5 million, it has generated no new housing and, including staff, only 133 jobs, of which only twenty can be directly attributed to USEDC. Even assuming 133 employees, which is probably greatly overstated, less than four-tenths of 1 percent of the population would be directly affected. The data for the other CDCs reflect the same situation—even for Bedford-Stuyvesant, which serves a population approaching one-half million people.

Even though this work is concerned primarily with an analysis of whether the CDC concept is a viable response to poverty, and not with which CDCs are responding well and which badly, the failure of CDCs to improve the quality of life for the poor people forces the question of why. The answer provides a conclusion to our analysis.

Those who advocate community economic development as a way of improving the quality of life for the poor often compare ghetto development to that of the Third World and suggest that the basic problem is the same. For example, they imply that both the ghetto and the Third World countries develop industry, balance imports and exports, bring in new trade, develop and improve technology, and the like. The problem is that the ghettos of this country have negative, and not positive, resources. Ghetto resources have been spent, and all that remains is human and physical liabilities.

In discussing economic development for the ghetto, one generally thinks of acquiring or starting new retail businesses, either by bringing in or starting labor-intensive industrial ventures or by engaging in property development.

In the case of retail ventures, it must be remembered that most of the larger efforts have left or are leaving the ghetto areas. They are leaving because the income levels of these areas are not sufficient to support the high cost of doing business, because their stores are mostly outdated and they do not believe that physical improvements and new equipment are feasible, and because the climate for business is untenable. These same factors are present for the CDC, and that is how they can point to a marginal business, one that is merely surviving, as a success.

Establishing an industry is as tenuous as starting a retail effort. One of the reasons that both large and small corporations have left the inner city is that the factory buildings in which they were housed have become obsolete. In most industries, the multi-story factory has given way to the single-story, single-direction, production flow concept. These buildings require a great deal of space not available in the inner city. Add to this the lack of optimum transportation facilities, higher insurance rates and land costs, environmental factors, employee preferences, and the personal preferences and home locations of the executives making the decision, and the reasons for fewer factories in the inner city become obvious. Again, these same factors affect the CDC and pose extremely difficult hurdles. In addition, the new CDC corporation must find management with experience, and if possible, from the area, or at least, in the case of most CDCs, someone black. This is not an easy accomplishment, as is demonstrated by the fact that the percentage of managers from the target areas is relatively small. Of all CDC efforts, those involving manufacturing have been least successful. Yet, from the employment standpoint, these offer the best possibilities.

Development of the physical assets of the community and involvement in other real estate activities are other potential directions for CDCs. These, of course, provide little employment other than that indirectly resulting from any rehabilitation effort or new construction effort. Of the CDCs profiled in this work, only Harlem Commonwealth has been successful in developing office buildings, although USEDC owns and leases the health center building and Bedford-Stuyvesant has Sheffield Center. The Harlem building, a seven-story office building, leases to city agencies, includes subsidiary operations, and houses its own offices. Other CDCs have little hope of duplicating such an effort, for the same reason business opportunities are few. The ghetto environment is not attractive to business, and one must attract business if money is to be earned in this type of property development. USEDC tried to purchase and find tenants for an office building, but without success. With tenants occupying the building at the time of option, USEDC had only to find tenants for one floor to make the purchase feasible; i.e., a breakeven proposition. USEDC appealed to both business and government but to no avail. The Hough area in Cleveland has many vacant usable office buildings, but the Hough Area Development Corporation evidently has not found them feasible for investment purposes.

Other property development activities, such as shopping centers, housing projects, and apartment buildings, have also proven economically not viable. Inner-city shopping centers have not been successful mostly because of the level of income found in the inner city. Apartment buildings have the same problem, and since the demise of FHA 235 and FHA 236 housing, housing projects are at a standstill.

All of these data indicate that the very concept of CDC is untenable, just as they suggest that private sector involvement is an irrationality. As shown in Chapters 4 and 5, the benefits derived by the poor are minimal. Therefore, the question remains: Who benefits from the CDC?

To the extent that there are benefits, middle- and upper-middle class Americans, along with large corporations, receive most of them. An average of only 28 percent of the managers are residents of the target areas. (See Chapter 4.) The employees largely represent middle-class professionals. In addition, the OEO personnel, auditing firms, and many other consulting groups benefit from the Special Impact Program. Profiting, too, are all the real estate firms selling or leasing property to the CDCs, the individuals and companies divesting themselves of their holdings (mostly tenuous) when CDCs acquire existing businesses, and the many firms that do business with the fledgling ventures. For example, of USEDC's $110,000 investment in Masco Products, $50,000 went directly to the former owners and the rest went for operating capital. In the case of the USEDC supermarket, $156,000 was invested, of which $40,000 went immediately to Wetterau

Corporation for inventory. Subsequently, the store lost $50,000 in the first ten weeks of operation, and Wetterau had gross sales for that period of $227,464. So it is easy to understand that others benefit more than the poor from the capital grants emanating from Washington.

One other benefit expected from the creation of CDCs in special impact areas is the stabilization of those areas. The initial planning for the CDC program resulted from an OEO staff assignment to develop a response to the Presidential Riot Commission Report.[4] There is no way to measure the extent of cooptation resulting from the CDC movement, but there can be no doubt that it basically maintains the system. According to Alan Altshuler, "it has the effect of legitimizing the system in the eyes of the blacks," or, for that matter, the poor who are propagandized through the program. Even here failure is evident because continued inner-city deterioration will cause new leaders to emerge as disillusionment increases.

CDC FUTURE

On January 4, 1975, President Ford signed into law the Community Services Act of 1974, which replaced the Office of Economic Opportunity with the Community Services Administration. In addition, a reorganization plan was submitted to create a new Community Economic Development Administration located in the Department of Commerce.

These changes are only organizational and administrative. Other changes that are taking place relate to policy and program philosophy and are more subtle and vastly more telling. These changes have resulted partly from pressure and influence from the National Congress of Community Economic Development and partly from the OEO staff's awareness that the past performance of CDCs has not been successful. Therefore, the emphasis on jobs, training, and community control is being replaced by an emphasis on maximization of profits and institution-building.

A policy statement from OEO in October 1974, provides some insight into its shifting attitudes. On profits, the statement reads: "Although it is appropriate for a given CDC to have a mix of venture types, the priority over the short term should be on business ventures. Moreover, among business ventures, the priority over the short term should be on profit maximization, rather than optimization." This simply means that ventures should not, at this time, be concerned with social objectives at the expense of some profit, but rather should look to profit only.

In relation to institution-building, the same policy statement indicated that institution-building "is and will remain, the top priority." "A wide range of institutions are needed, including planning and coordinating institutions, capital-providing and debt-providing institutions, employment-generating and wage-increasing institutions." Between the lines one can read the suggestion that greater coordination should be set up with established outside forces to provide a surer investment route before future investments are committed.

Statements on employment policy are even more provoking because they run counter to previous CDC policy; yet, they follow what has actually been evolving within the movement.

> While the employment of low-income and unemployed impact area residents and increased income for impact area residents are among the most important long-range objectives of the Special Impact Program, it is not anticipated that any CDC can make a significant impact over the short term in this area. . . .

> All things being equal, ventures with a greater employment potential should be given higher priority than those with smaller employment potential, but in the short term job creation should not be pursued as an objective at the sacrifice of venture profits. . . .

> While human development objectives are essential to increased incomes and improved quality of life, misplaced emphasis at the early stages of a CDC's efforts may, in the absence of specific subsidies for that purpose, detract from venture performance and threaten the institution-building priorities of the CDC. Investment in training venture managers, rather than the recruitment of expert managers, has been a major cause of CDC venture loss to date. . . .

> In order to produce benefits for low-income impact area residents, however, the institution-building and venture development efforts of the CDC require the participation of the non-poor in managerial and leadership roles.[5]

It would seem, then, that the OED staff is determined to view the CDC as a purely profit-seeking effort, "in the short run," and that it views the supposed benefits of community control and community participation as what they have always been: rhetoric. In OEO's 1975 review of USEDC, it noted that too many residents were on the board and that USEDC should seek more participation from outside business sources. It also stated that, while attempts at upward mobility for staff members were commendable, USEDC should seek more qualified and business-oriented staff members.

CDC's future direction will be toward more, not less, outside non-resident participation; employment of fewer, not more, residents; and a greater exploitative, not a more cooperative, role. Therefore, in a sense, rather than new rulers in the ghetto, there will arise representatives of the same "old rulers" perceived as "new rulers."

Once the CDCs recognize that business development is beyond their reach, they will more and more turn to physical development. At the moment, all USEDC efforts are being concentrated on dismantling existing businesses and starting housing and apartment building rehabilitation projects. Rehabilitation of the Sherwood Courts Apartments has begun, and attempts are being made to rehabilitate single-family units on a scattered-site basis. In the case of Sherwood Courts, the rent structure is projected for middle-income and upper middle-income tenants. The scattered-site program is to be directed toward the federal rent subsidy program, Section 8 of the 1974 Housing and Community Development Act, and therefore is for lower income family housing. It remains to be seen whether they can rehabilitate single-family units at a cost low enough to be supported by housing subsidy rent structures.

It seems obvious that the CDCs are turning to physical development in a final attempt to anchor themselves as permanent community institutions. Through property ownership, they hope to create an income base that will at least support their salaries, if not provide profits for reinvestment. It is believed that credibility with lending institutions and local power structures can be developed through these efforts, and that, if they can survive long enough for the national economy to turn around, they will benefit from the overall economic improvement. At that time, it is thought, they can reenter the business development phase.

Will conditions really change for the CDCs? The answer is probably no. Their past failures will only intensify private sector beliefs that the ghetto is no place to do business. Forced to conduct physical development activities within the framework of the free enterprise system, the CDCs will not be able to meet the needs of poor people, and it is doubtful that they will attract tenants able to pay the rents needed to make the programs viable.

CDCs have not been able to attract the private sector, upon which their success depends. Most important, they have not helped poor people, a failing which is reason enough to disband the organizations. The CDC concept should be set aside, funding should be denied, and the legislators should look for a new approach to improving the quality of life for the poor of the United States.

NOTES

1. Charles L. Dearing, et al., *The ABC of the NRA* (Washington, D.C.: The Brookings Institution, 1934), p. 32.

2. Barry Stein, *Rebuilding Bedford-Stuyvesant* (Cambridge, Mass.: Center for Community Economic Development, 1975).

3. "The Uphill Road to Black Capitalism," *Nation's Business,* December 1970.

4. Stewart Perry, *Federal Support for CDCs* (Cambridge, Mass.: Center for Community Economic Development, 1973), p. 8.

5. Office of Economic Opportunity, "Policy Statement on Special Impact Program," October 1974.

EPILOGUE

One of the most disturbing aspects of the CDC movement is that it is defined and generally accepted as a new approach to poverty, when in fact it is nothing more than the traditional Anglo-American welfare program. It is the kind of self-help welfare that has been given since Elizabeth I of England. As has been the case for centuries, self-help and equal opportunity have been the nemesis of the poor.

Equally problematic has been the practice of designing programs for the benefit of discreet groups; i.e., the poor or the black. These programs are self-defeating because of their failure to gain the support of the majority, who support neither the poor nor the black. It would seem then that the best approach would be to devise programs dealing with specific societal *needs* rather than specific societal groups. It is also time to reject the rhetoric and mythology of equal opportunity and begin to look at the possibilities of *equality of condition.*

In essence, the United States should become more system-oriented and direct its efforts and resources toward correcting the system's flaws. This effort can begin by including all of the people in American society and by once and for all putting a halt to the insane penchant for categorizing. Instead of health delivery for the poor, there should be health delivery for the total society—a delivery system that will be the same for all. In the same way, there should be housing standards below which nothing will be permitted, transportation systems that will make all citizens mobile to the extent necessary in a modern society, and education for all of our children equally.

It is time we realized that providing opportunities to work, providing some money on a "less eligibility" basis, will not alleviate poverty. We must deliver to society the categorical needs of society by changing and improving the systems that control delivery.

This transformation has no more been accomplished through the "New Federalism" than it was through the "War on Poverty." The New Federalism was designed to return control to local governments by returning to them a portion of their tax moneys for purposes appropriate to local control. The programs were often said to assist poor people. Thus it was that the CDC found ready acceptance with proponents of the New Federalism. It was a program purported to assist poor people, with the poor people themselves having control. Local control translates as the people, knowing better their own needs than anyone, deciding what programs should be developed and how money should be spent. In actual practice, the example of the CDC shows that self-interest groups determine what programs will be developed and how money will be spent, with little concern for the needs of the local population.

On a different level, revenue-sharing funds are being used to augment existing local services, which benefit that portion of the population not considered poor, and that revenue-sharing funds have not been expended for the needs of poor people. The following are some examples of what has occurred under the auspices of the New Federalism. In St. Louis County, Missouri, the county supervisor attempted to spend the revenue-sharing funds to build a new golf course, which would obviously benefit only the affluent. Block grants under the 1974 Housing and Community Development Act are being expended to improve central business districts and to build roads and sewers, with little or no money going to provide new housing or new housing opportunities for the poor. The New Federalism placed the decision for the expenditure of funds—presumably funds that would assist poor people—in the hands of self-interest groups across the country who eagerly lined their own pockets by using the funds mostly to support their own business interests. For example, the money was spent on streets and sewers developing business areas or redevelopment areas rather than in the poverty areas. While block grant funds for community development are supposed to improve housing or economic opportunities for the poor, they are in fact spent to benefit business interests. The rationale of course, is that it will create more jobs for the poor via the "trickle-down system."

Control should be taken away from local oligarchies and should revert to the federal government. The myth of effective localism, along with state rights, should be destroyed once and for all. National programs should be established to improve the quality of life for all citizens; these programs should encompass education, health service, transportation, housing, day care centers, the elderly, and criminal and penal code. Only if our systems meet the needs of the total society will poor people, especially the poor black people, benefit substantially.

The following are meant as strategic, rather than tactical, alternatives, and as such are not intended as suggested programs. These examples represent positions significantly different from past and present approaches to social programs in the United States.

In a recent meeting on the American city and where it was headed, I heard an urbanologist state that the most liberating factor in modern society is the automobile. The automobile, he stated, has given modern man mobility and freedom of choice, particularly in regards to his residence and place of work. This kind of mentality has been responsible for road-building legislation that has effectively imprisoned the poor black in the inner-city ghetto. The automobile has liberated affluent America, while placing a greater burden on the poor and impeding their progress, because it has brought about the demise of public transportation. In order to find employment, the poor must now have an automobile. The cost of maintaining a car further impoverishes the poor person, so that even with employment the condition of his life fails to improve. Cheap public transportation for local travel, such as a street car system, could eliminate the need for the automobile. A national system of railroads modeled on the European system would further reduce the need for automobiles and relegate them to the position of luxury, where they belong. Real freedom of choice and real mobility would then accrue to the total society rather than what we now have: mobility and freedom for some, and slavery to the demands of the automobile or imprisonment in the ghetto for others.

At present there exists no federal public housing program for the poor in the United States. It is appalling that the only operable program for poverty housing is a housing subsidy program whose success depends on the participation of the private sector and the ability of the poor to negotiate for housing. With a decreasing housing stock, especially in cities where demolition has been adopted as a remedy for social problems (the so-called urban renewal), and an increasing population, supply and demand removes housing beyond the reach of subsidy programs. The United States should move away from the concept of private homeownership to a concept of safe, sanitary, and appropriate housing for all provided by the state, as necessary. In Great Britain, over 30 percent of the housing stock is owned by the state, while in the United States only 2 percent is state-owned. Furthermore, state-owned or public housing in the United States is mostly clustered in the impacted poverty areas of our large cities. What is needed in all our communities is scattered-site public housing, both single-unit and multiple-unit. Unless we accomplish economically, socially, and racially integrated communities, a large portion of our population will be condemned to a life unsatisfactory for humans, life in which the poor are forced together and in which, being powerless, they are denied basic human services. Through social, economic, and racial integration, all communities would demand satisfactory services and would have adequate power to get what they demanded. Other than elitism and prejudice, there is no reason why public housing should be relegated to single areas, particularly areas impacted by the poor. Through enlightened housing policies, existing housing stock that is structurally sound could be rehabilitated and the present programs of demolition halted. For our cities to become healthy entities once again, all that is deteriorating should be renewed, new housing should be built, and a socioeconomic mix be provided.

In education, our system furthers inequality by making the quality of education available dependent on the local community tax base. An affluent community has greater resources and can therefore offer better quality education than can a poor community. In most cases, the inner-city schools are overcrowded and understaffed, and are housed in inadequate buildings. A national program could strive for equality in dollars spent per student, in number of students per teacher, and in facility allocation. It would also assure opportunities for standardizing programs and for better teacher assignments. These methods alone would not completely eliminate inequality in education, but the country would at last be pointing in the right direction.

Health care is another important area. The piecemeal approach recommended by different legislators will never effectively change health care service. So long as the medical profession retains control of health care and the fee system for medical treatment remains in force, the quality differential for health care will persist. Many areas of the country have a severe shortage of medical doctors and facilities. Unless a national health service is developed to provide health service according to need rather than market demand and ability to pay, inequalities will continue. These inequalities lessen the quality of life for lower income families, especially among blacks.

A change in the national attitude toward the poor is urgently needed. The answer provided by the CDC and by the New Federalism—self-help and community control—will only transfer the problems of the poor to other shoulders. The federal government must now face the fact that only programs of national dimension will alter the life of poor people in the United States.

BIBLIOGRAPHY

BOOKS AND DISSERTATIONS

Agee, James, and Walker Evans. *Let Us Now Praise Famous Men.*
New York: Ballantine Books, 1966.

Allen, Robert L. *Black Awakening in Capitalist America.* New York:
Doubleday and Co., Inc., 1969.

Altshuler, Alan A. *Community Control: The Black Demand for Participation in Large American Cities.* New York: Pegasus, 1970.

Aptheker, Herbert, ed. *The Education of Black People: Ten Critiques,
1906-1960, By W. E. B. DuBois.* Amherst: University of Massachusetts
Press, 1973.

Aschrott, P. F. *The English Poor Law System.* London: Knight and Co.,
1902.

Bennett, Jerome, Jr. *Before the Mayflower: A History of the Negro in America.* Chicago: Johnson Publication Co., Inc., 1966.

Bentley, George R. *A History of the Freedmen's Bureau.* New York: Octagon Books, 1970.

Berle, Adolf, Jr. *Power Without Property.* New York: Harcourt, Brace and Co., 1959.

Brann, W. Paul, et al. *Community Economic Development Efforts: Five Case Studies.* New York: Committee for Economic Development, 1964.

Bremner, Robert H. *American Philanthropy.* Chicago: University of Chicago Press, 1960.

Carus-Wilson, Eleanor Mary. *Essays in Economic History.* Vol. III. E. M. Wilson, ed. London: Edward Arnold Ltd., 1962.

Cronon, Edmund David. *Black Moses.* Madison: University of Wisconsin Press, 1969.

Cyert, Richard M., and James G. March. *A Behavioral Theory of the Firm.* Englewood Cliffs, N.J.: Prentice-Hall, Inc., 1963.

Dahrendorf, Rolf. *Class and Class Conflict in Industrial Society.* Stanford, Calif.: Stanford University Press, 1959.

Dearing, Charles L., et al. *The ABC of the NRA.* Washington, D.C.: The Brookings Institution, 1934.

Drucker, Peter F. *The Age of Discontinuity.* New York: Harper and Row, 1969.

_____. *The Practice of Management.* New York: Harper and Row, 1957.

DuBois, W. E. B. *Darkwater.* New York: Schocken Books, 1969.

_____. *The Souls of Black Folk.* Greenwich, Conn.: Fawcett Publications, Inc., 1961.

Faux, Geoffrey. *CDCs: New Hope for the Inner City.* New York: The Twentieth Century Fund, 1971.

Fox, Elton C. *Garvey.* New York: Dodd, Mead and Co., 1972.

Friedman, Milton. *Capitalism and Freedom.* Chicago: University of Chicago Press, 1962.

Galbraith, John Kenneth. *The Great Crash.* Cambridge, Mass.: Houghton Mifflin Co., 1954.

_____. *The New Industrial State.* New York: American Library, Inc., 1968.

Garvey, A. J., ed. *The Philosophy and Opinion of Marcus Garvey.* New York: Universal Publishing House, 1923.

Garvey, Amy Jacques. *Garvey and Garveyism*. London: Collier-MacMillan, Ltd., 1963.

Gilmore, Donald R. *Developing the Little Economies*. New York: Committee for Economic Development, 1960.

Gouldner, Alvin W. *The Coming Crises of Western Sociology*. New York: Aran Books, 1970.

Grant, Joanne, ed. *Black Protest*. Greenwich, Conn.: Fawcett Publications, Inc., 1970.

Gruen, Victor, and Larry Smith. *Shopping Towns, USA*. New York: Von Nostrand and Reinhold, 1960.

Haddad, William, and Douglas Pugh, eds. *Black Economic Development*. Englewood Cliffs, N.J.: Prentice-Hall, 1969.

Hampden-Turner, Charles. *From Poverty to Dignity*. Garden City, N.Y.: Anchor Books, 1975.

Harlan, Louis R., and John W. Blessingame, eds. *The Booker T. Washington Papers*. Vol. 1. Chicago: University of Illinois Press, 1972.

Heffner, William C. *Poor Laws–Pennsylvania*. Cleona, Penn.: Holzapful Publishing Co., 1913.

Henderson, William L., and Larry Ledebur. *Economic Disparity: Problems and Strategies for Black America*. New York: Free Press, 1970.

Hoover, Herbert. *The New Day, Campaign Speeches of Herbert Hoover, 1928*. Stanford, Calif.: Stanford University Press, 1928.

Kerner, Otto. *Report of the National Advisory Commission on Civil Disorders*. New York: Bantam Books, 1968.

Logan, Rayford W., ed. *W. E. B. DuBois: A Profile*. New York: Hill and Wang, 1971.

Mannheim, Karl. *Man and Society in an Age of Reconstruction*. New York: Harcourt, Brace and Co., 1940.

Marx, Karl. *Das Capital*. New York: Modern Library, 1906.

Mathew, Victoria Earl, ed. *Black Belt Diamonds: Gems from the Speeches, Addresses and Talks to Students of Booker T. Washington*. New York: Negro University Press, 1969.

Mencher, Samuel. *Poor Law to Poverty Program*. Pittsburgh, Penn.: Pittsburgh University Press, 1967.

Newbeck, Kenneth John. "Social Responsibility and the American Corporation: A Benefit-Cost Perspective." Ph.D. Dissertation, Washington University, 1972.

Pease, William H., and Jane H. Pease. *Black Utopia: Negro Communal Experiments in America.* Madison: The State Historical Society of Wisconsin, 1963.

Piven, Frances Fox, and Richard A. Cloward. *Regulating the Poor: The Functions of Public Welfare.* New York: Random House, 1971.

Rivera Jose. "Community Control of Economic Development Planning: A Study of the Recipient Beneficiaries of Change as the Actors of Change." Ph.D. Dissertation, Brandeis University, 1972.

Rollins, Alfred B., Jr., ed. *Depression, Recovery, and War 1929-1945.* New York: McGraw-Hill, 1966.

Romasco, Albert V. *The Poverty of Abundance.* New York: Oxford University Press, 1965.

Shonfield, Andrew. *Modern Capitalism.* New York: Oxford University Press, 1967.

Steiner, George A. *Top Management Planning.* New York: Macmillan Co., 1969.

Tabb, William K. *The Political Economy of the Black Ghetto.* New York: W. W. Norton and Co., Inc., 1970.

Thompson, E. P. *The Making of the English Working Class.* New York: Vintage Books, 1963.

Veblen, Thorstein. *The Engineers and the Price System.* New York: Reprints of Economic Classics, 1965.

Vincent, Theodore G. *Black Power and the Garvey Movement.* Berkeley, Calif.: Ramparts Press, 1971.

Washington, Booker T. *The Negro in Business.* New York: AMS Press, 1971.

————, and W. E. B. DuBois. *The Negro in the South.* New York: Citadel Press, 1970.

Woods, Robert, et al. *The Poor in Great Cities.* New York: Charles Scribner's Sons, 1895.

ARTICLES

Calloway, Ernest. "Who Runs St. Louis and How." *The St. Louis American.* October 18, 1973.

Center for Community Economic Development. "Profile: Harlem Commonwealth Council." *Newsletter.* May 1974.

_____. "Profile: Bedford-Stuyvesant." *Newsletter*. December 1973.

_____. "Special Impact Program Policy Statement." *Newsletter*. November 1974.

Galbraith, John Kenneth. "What Comes After General Motors." *The New Republic*. November 2, 1974.

Green, Gerson, and Geoffrey Faux. "The Social Utility of Black Enterprise." *Black Economic Development*. William Haddad and Douglas Pugh, eds. Englewood Cliffs, N.J.: Prentice Hall, 1969.

McCall, David B. "Profit: Spur for Solving Social Ills." *Harvard Business Review*. May-June 1973.

Millsaps, Betty. "New Roads to Economic Opportunity." *NAM Reports*. July 15, 1974.

New York Times, The. June 21, 1968.

Perry, Stewart E. "Black Institutions, Black Separatism and Ghetto Economic Development." *Human Organizations* 31, No. 3. Fall 1972.

_____. "National Policy and the Community Development Corporation." *Law and Contemporary Problems* (Duke University Law School). Spring 1971.

"Shattered Dreams: Black Leaders' Plans to Build Ghetto Stores Often End in Defeat." *The Wall Street Journal*. May 1, 1972.

Tobin, Gary Allen. "The St. Louis School Crisis: Population Shifts and Voting Patterns." St. Louis, Mo., Washington University Department of History. June 1970.

"Uphill Road to Black Capitalism, The." *Nation's Business*. December 1970.

DOCUMENTS

Abt Associates, Inc. *An Evaluation of the Special Impact Program*. Final Report. December, 1973.

Congressional Record, July 24, 1968, January 15, 1969, June 9, 1971.

Ford Foundation Policy Paper. *Community Development Corporation: A Strategy for Depressed Urban and Rural Areas*. New York. May 1973.

Kelly, Rita Mae. *The Executive Directors of CDCs*. Cambridge, Mass.: Center for Community Economic Development, 1974.

Macphee, John. *Local Government and Community Autonomy in East Boston*. Cambridge, Mass.: Center for Community Economic Development, 1973.

National Advisory Council on Economic Development. *Sixth Annual Report.* 1973.

Perry, Stewart. *Federal Support for CDCs.* Cambridge, Mass.: Center for Community Economic Development, 1973.

St. Louis City Planning Commission. *The Workable Program for Community Improvement.* May 1974.

Stein, Barry. *Rebuilding Bedford-Stuyvesant.* Cambridge, Mass.: Center for Community Economic Development, 1975.

Union Sarah Economic Development Corporation. *Proposal for Special Impact Program 1.* June 1969.

Westinghouse Learning Corporation. *Evaluation of the Special Impact Program.* July 1970. (OEO Contract Number B 89-4532.)

INDEX